THE
GOD
POCKET™

THE
GOD
POCKET™

**He owns it. You carry it.
Suddenly, everything changes.**

BRUCE
WILKINSON

AUTHOR OF THE *NEW YORK TIMES* BESTSELLER *THE PRAYER OF JABEZ*
WITH DAVID KOPP

MULTNOMAH
BOOKS

THE GOD POCKET
PUBLISHED BY MULTNOMAH BOOKS
12265 Oracle Boulevard, Suite 200
Colorado Springs, Colorado 80921

Every story in this book is an account of an actual event. In a few cases, minor details have been modified slightly to improve readability or to protect privacy. The concept of the God Pocket was introduced briefly in a previous book, *You Were Born for This.*

ISBN 978-1-60142-185-2
ISBN 978-1-60142-186-9 (electronic)

Copyright © 2011 by Exponential Inc.

Cover design by Kristopher K. Orr

Published in the United States by WaterBrook Multnomah, an imprint of the Crown Publishing Group, a division of Random House Inc., New York.

MULTNOMAH and its mountain colophon are registered trademarks of Random House Inc.

Library of Congress Cataloging-in-Publication Data
Wilkinson, Bruce.
   The God pocket : he owns it, you carry it : suddenly, everything changes / Bruce Wilkinson with David Kopp. — 1st ed.
      p. cm.
   Includes bibliographical references (p.   ).
   ISBN 978-1-60142-185-2 — ISBN 978-1-60142-186-9 (electronic)
   1. Christian stewardship. 2. Money—Religious aspects—Christianity. 3. Charity. I. Kopp, David, 1949- II. Title.
   BV772.W48 2011
   248'.6—dc23

                                   2011028975

Printed in the United States of America
2011—First Edition

10 9 8 7 6 5 4 3 2 1

SPECIAL SALES
Most WaterBrook Multnomah books are available at special quantity discounts when purchased in bulk by corporations, organizations, and special-interest groups. Custom imprinting or excerpting can also be done to fit special needs. For information, please e-mail SpecialMarkets@WaterBrookMultnomah.com or call 1-800-603-7051.

INVITATION

What if you could take a little something out of your pocket today that would make God visible—and then give that little something to another person you just met?

Of course, I'm asking you to imagine a shocking idea, but I'm completely serious.

Picture the moment. You strike up a conversation with a passerby outside a restaurant, or someone you've just met in the mall, or a newcomer in your church lobby. Suddenly you realize this is the moment. You smile at your new acquaintance, reach into your pocket, then lean forward. The other person doesn't suspect a thing. But before they know what's happening, you press into their hands the very presence and touch of our loving God.

Stay with me.

Now imagine that this person *only minutes earlier* had been secretly calling out to God for help, for an answer, for any shred of evidence that Heaven even noticed their crisis.

And then you showed up! There you are, placing (so to speak) an enormous ball of light into the hands of the person who has been standing alone in the dark for days. Or years.

Wouldn't that be something?

Assuming for a minute you could do such a thing, that one experience would change your life. Wouldn't it?

This book is about a mysterious little idea that's almost too big for words.

The joy would be contagious. And you'd be so lit up inside with your own happiness that everyone would notice. Years later you'd still be talking about it.

And imagine the impact on the person who, out of the blue, received what you had to share. They'd see their life and their future differently from that day on. They'd feel very differently about God too.

This book is about a mysterious little idea that's almost too big for words. Sure, you don't exactly pull our mighty, living God out of your pocket or purse. But it feels very, very close to that. You'll see. It's happened countless times for me and for thousands of others who have said yes to the God Pocket. If you're willing to try it, you'll know it was God who showed up to touch your heart and meet an urgent need in someone else's life.

And you'll be in a rush to say yes to another God Pocket adventure soon.

I hope you turn the page.

THE GOD POCKET

He owns it. You carry it. Suddenly, everything changes!

Contents

1. HEAVEN LEANS DOWN 1

   What happens when God makes Himself
   visible through you

2. HOW THE GOD POCKET WORKS 15

   Seven steps that prepare you to partner
   with God for a financial miracle

3. WAS THAT A NUDGE? 35

   How God leads you to the person He wants
   to bless with your God Pocket

4. AGENTS IN ACTION 55

   Your job description for successful
   God Pocket deliveries

5. THE MYSTERY OF MULTIPLYING 75

   God's surprising plan to replenish your
   resources when you give

6. The Generosity Conspiracy 97
Stories of God's "little people" who are
reaching for very big things

7. Your Next Step.................. 115
Now is the moment. Heaven waits.
Will you make your move?

Acknowledgments 125
Notes........................ 127
Welcome to God Pocket
Partners! 129

Heaven Leans Down

What happens when God makes
Himself visible through you

This God Pocket story starts at the counter of a pharmacy in South Carolina at two in the afternoon. A young husband is there to pick up a prescription for his wife. The cashier gives him back his change, then hands him the prescription. "Thanks," he says, and he turns to go.

That's when the young man freezes. He's staring down at his change to be sure of what he's seeing. But he *is* sure.

The cashier has returned incorrect change. Too much. A lot too much, actually.

Have you ever found yourself in such a circumstance? Most of us have.

All of this happens in seconds, of course. But here's the thing: The young husband is out of work—laid off like a lot of other folks when the economy fell apart. It's been a while now, and he and his wife are getting desperate. Then today he gets this lucky break—finally!—and it's really going to help. Groceries, some breathing room, maybe a little something for his wife (he can already see her smile).

But then again…

The young man's heart sinks. And sinks some more. "Ma'am," he says. It's so hard for him to get the word out.

The cashier glances up from her next customer, wondering what his problem is.

"Ma'am, I think you gave me the wrong change," he says.

Sure enough, she did. Quickly she takes back the extra. "Sorry," she says.

By the time he walks out of the pharmacy, his heart is down in his shoes. He did what was right, but he still feels like he lost. Like he's a permanent loser. Out in the parking lot, he climbs dejectedly into his old red pickup and hands the prescription to his wife.

That little drama at the cash register? He can't bring himself to mention it.

"I'VE BEEN CARRYING AROUND SOME OF GOD'S MONEY"

At the same time, across town a woman is driving toward Kentucky Fried Chicken. She's on an emergency mission—to buy a bag of hot-sauce packets. Not a bite of lunch or even a drink, mind you. Just KFC hot sauce. Her name is Darlene, and she's my lovely wife (and that's how I know what happened). You see, we were about to embark on a speaking tour of South Africa, where our son David currently lives. When she asked him what he'd like us to bring for him, he immediately came out with, "Kentucky Fried Chicken hot sauce!"

Some things you just can't explain.

At KFC, Darlene walks up to Margie, the woman behind the counter, and delivers her unusual order. Margie's eyebrows shoot up. Apparently people don't often stop by for whole bags of hot-sauce packets. The manager goes in the back to fill Darlene's order, and since business is slow, Darlene and Margie begin talking. It doesn't take long for Darlene to discover that Margie is struggling financially and very discouraged.

"I remembered that I had placed several bills in my God Pocket the week before," Darlene told me later. "I took one out, folded it, and taking her hand, quietly placed the bill there. I told her, 'Just something to remind you that God knows your situation and wants you to be encouraged today.'"

Apparently, customers don't often do that kind of thing either at KFC. Maybe never, because right away Margie's eyes fill with tears. "You just have no idea—," she begins. But before the two can talk further, a twenty-something customer enters, steps up to the counter, and puts in her order.

"How much for a glass of water?" she asks.

Darlene glances at Margie. "You charge for water here?"

"Restaurants have to pay for the cup," Margie explains. Then to the young woman, "Thirty-seven cents."

The customer rummages in her purse and finally plunks a quarter on the counter. "I have to take some medicine," she says wearily. Then her shoulders sag. "I guess I only have a quarter."

Do you see what's going on here in South Carolina a little after two in the afternoon?

What Darlene sees is God at work. Smiling, she asks the young woman to let her buy the water for her, and she does. The young woman gives her a quiet thank-you in return, takes the water and her quarter from the counter, and hurries out.

A minute later Darlene is walking out of the restaurant too, carrying her bag of Africa-bound hot-sauce packets. But in her heart she's trying to make sense of her recent encounters. *Lord,* she prays, *I haven't helped anyone in need with my God Pocket for weeks, and then today You place two people in my path. I wish I had responded faster and given that young woman the money left in my God Pocket.*

I took one out, folded it, and taking her hand, quietly placed the bill there. I told her, "Just something to remind you that God knows your situation and wants you to be encouraged today."

She has already gotten into her car when she notices that she is parked next to a red pickup. Seated on the pickup's passenger side is the young woman. In her hand she holds the cup of water. Right away Darlene realizes that Heaven has given her another chance.

Here's how she described to me what happened next:

"With the bills from my God Pocket in hand, I opened my car door and gently tapped on her window. When she lowered it, I asked if she would do me a favor. 'I've been carrying around some of God's money,' I said, 'and I believe He would like me to give it to you.' That was all. Then I handed her the money."

You can imagine the young woman's surprise. She catches her breath. Her hand flies to her mouth. She can't begin to explain what is happening. But if you've been following this story carefully, maybe you can.

Only then does Darlene look across at the young man behind the steering wheel. He is staring at the money in his wife's hand, and tears are starting to roll down his cheeks. "You're not...going to believe this," he says.

And he proceeds to tell Darlene their story. (Did you see this coming?) He had lost his job, times were tough, and just a few blocks away, when he'd gone for his wife's medicine, the cashier had given him back too much money by mistake. At first it had seemed like a huge provision, but the money didn't belong to him, so he had returned it. What a struggle that had been!

The young husband leans over to his wife. He can barely get the words out. But this is what he says: "Look at this! God used someone we don't even know to bless us with far more than I gave back!"

HOW WE SEE THE WORLD

Think back over your life. Have you had your own experience where Heaven seemed to plant you squarely in the crossroads of somebody's life and—in that place, in that moment, you just *knew* that you'd been specially sent? And then God showed up in an amazing way. Ever since, you've been filled with gratitude that, out of all the people in the universe that day, God picked you.

What if God is inviting you into those kinds of experiences on a regular basis? Actually, there are a lot of reasons why He would, but here's a big one:

You and I see the world differently than many do. We look out the window and see God. Not in physical form, but left and right we see evidence of His presence. We see His steadfast faithfulness all through the story of our lives,

working for our good in the wonderful ups and the difficult downs. We open the Word and experience His loving
guidance. We look in the faces of our children and see
amazing grace.

Not always, but usually.

But for a lot of folks, it's not like that at all. They look
out the window and don't see
any sign that God is real or
that He cares. They look at
the story of their lives and see
a lonely, disappointing jour-
ney. They have long since
decided that if God is some-
where about, He must be otherwise occupied, because
when they call, He doesn't seem to answer.

How does God break into our material world to touch troubled individuals with His great love?

You might say that, for some people in our world,
God's reputation is in trouble.

Let me ask you this: When Heaven leans down to
make God "visible" in someone's life—maybe yours—
how does that happen? How does God break into our
material world to touch troubled individuals with His
great love and show them His personal attention?

At a KFC in South Carolina one ordinary afternoon, God took four people by surprise and revealed Himself to each of them in tangible, unforgettable ways. Could anyone but God have brought it all together so perfectly?

Consider:

- A young, unemployed husband struggles to return an overpayment to a cashier. When no one else knows, God knows what it is costing him to do the right thing.

- God knows the young couple's need and seeks to meet it. Most of all, I think, He longs for them to know that He is with them in their trials and that He cares. But how can He get the message to them?

- Across town, Margie, the KFC employee, is secretly struggling too. God knows. He wants to encourage her and show her how deeply He cares.

- Enter Darlene, prepared on a moment's notice to be God's representative. Of course, after that phone call from Africa, what's on her mind is...hot sauce. Why? God knows that

Darlene, who wouldn't ordinarily stop by Kentucky Fried Chicken at two in the afternoon, wouldn't hesitate to go there at any hour for a bag of hot-sauce packets if that's what her son said he really wanted.

- At that exact moment, God brings Margie, the young wife, and Darlene together. God knows what's about to happen, but do they? Not on your life!

- In quick succession, two "out of the blue," God-arranged encounters follow. Darlene reaches into her God Pocket to bless Margie and into her purse to buy water for the young wife.

- But God is not finished. He sets up a third "out of the blue" encounter at the window of the couple's truck, where Darlene again reaches into her God Pocket to bless the young wife and her husband. Was that almost-missed appointment a mistake? I don't think so, because Darlene got to see firsthand why God's provision through her was so special—and so miraculous—for the young couple in need.

Talk about a God moment! Only God could have arranged such "chance" encounters that led to very real physical and emotional needs being met. And that is what He did.

God was willing and able, and thankfully one of His servants was ready. And look what happened!

When Darlene was telling me about her encounter, she described the conversation with the young couple that followed as she stood by the truck. "We talked for a while about God's faithfulness and how He alone is our supplier and giver of every good and perfect gift. When I finally returned to my car and watched them drive away, my heart was overwhelmed with gratitude that God had given me the opportunity to see Him display His love for that precious couple."

She paused and then added, "Oh, and guess what? The manager gave me the bag of hot-sauce packets for free!"

By the time you finish this book

You might be wondering where all this is going.

For example, what exactly is a God Pocket? Where did the money in Darlene's God Pocket come from?

How would you or I know when to reach for it so that the miracle Heaven had in mind could actually happen through us?

In the pages ahead we'll explore these questions and more. Already it should be clear to you that the God Pocket prepares a person to deliver God's provision to someone in need. You can be that delivery person. By the time you finish this little book, you'll understand how to be in the right place at the right time to partner with Heaven in a God-arranged encounter. And you'll come away *knowing* God, not you, made it happen.

> The God Pocket has as much to do with God's deep desire to bless you as it does with His desire to bless others through you.

But let's begin with a couple of things you might not have figured out.

First, the God Pocket has as much to do with God's deep desire *to bless you* beyond anything you can imagine[1] as it does with His desire *to bless others through you*. Over and over again, the Bible declares that He's never desired anything less for you, and you honor Him by desiring nothing less for yourself.

And second, while the God Pocket is primarily a ministry with money, it's not your money.

You see, when you reach into your pocket or purse, you're not intending to give anything of yours away.

Curious how this could be possible? The next chapter will show you.

THE GOD POCKET
He owns it. You carry it. Suddenly, everything changes!

2

HOW THE GOD
POCKET WORKS

Seven steps that prepare you to partner
with God for a financial miracle

Most people I've talked to would give almost anything for
an experience like Darlene's. Wouldn't you? That afternoon God seemed to step right into the lives of four people
to reveal Himself.

A rare event, of course.

Maybe one of a kind.

You might be thinking that, for you, such a thing won't be happening anytime soon…

But what if God wanted to reveal His extravagant goodness to people in need, not just once or twice in a lifetime, but dozens if not hundreds of times? And since He *is* a God of infinite goodness and compassion, why wouldn't He?

Consider for a moment this shocking possibility: countless times every day our God deeply desires to meet the urgent needs of people all around us, but something or someone gets in the way.

In this chapter I will show you what that problem "something or someone" is (I think you'll be surprised). And then I'll show you a simple solution that will bring you almost as much delight as it brings God.

HOW GOD MOVES MONEY AROUND

Have you ever considered how God meets urgent financial needs on earth? I mean, how exactly does He go about that?

At a fund-raising banquet recently, a man at my table told me he had been at four different fund-raising events already that year. Every time he turned around, it seemed someone was asking for money for worthy projects. He talked about his frustration for a while, then got to the heart of the matter. "I just don't understand!" he blurted out. "Is God short on cash?"

I'll admit, it took me awhile to wrap my mind around the idea. He is Lord of all creation, after all. He owns the cattle on a thousand hills.[1] Psalm 24:1 declares, "The earth is the LORD's, and all its fullness." How could God have a cash problem?

But follow me as I trace how God moves money from His infinite store of wealth into a needy person's pocket. I think you'll see what I mean.

Let's begin with you. Let's say *you* are the one in desperate straits. Your situation has become so urgent that just hours ago you cried out to God for help. God heard your request and felt the awful panic in your heart.

> I just don't understand!" he blurted out. "Is God short on cash?"

Let's assume that His answer to your plea is yes. What will happen now? How, practically, is God going to get you the dollars that you need and that He desires to give you?

Common sense and a careful study of Scripture tell me that, with your situation, God might respond in one of three ways.

God might give it to you directly. He could make the money in Heaven and drop it out of the sky onto your kitchen table. *Wham!* One minute you're staring into your empty hands. The next you're looking at a stack of bills right in front of you.

He could. But will He?

Not likely. I find no instance in the Bible or in my life where God personally and directly delivered money to a person in need. Honestly, I'd strike out "not likely" and go with a plain "no."

God might send an angel. He has countless angels at His service. So He could direct an angel to bring you the exact provision that you need and that He wants you to have.

He could. But will He?

Again I'd have to say not likely. Television shows aside, I find nowhere in my experience or in Scripture that a spiritual being from Heaven shows up with cash in hand. We might pray and hope and dream that it will happen. I, for one, believe it *could* happen. But as far as I can tell, it doesn't happen. When it comes to money, God doesn't seem to work that way.

Unless I'm overlooking something, that leaves one option.

God can partner with a person. He did it with Darlene in South Carolina. He's done it in my life countless times. He does it every day through people all over the world. And He could do it to meet your need too.

My friend, this is how God *does* work. Yes, He is Lord of creation. Yes, He is all-powerful. But for reasons we can't completely understand, our God chooses to rely primarily on human partners to get funds to people in need.

It seems odd. But then again, hasn't God chosen to spread the gospel in the same way? He could have written John 3:16 across the sky in giant letters. Or put an angel at everybody's front door to announce the way of salvation. Instead, His good and perfect will is to depend on people to deliver the most important news in the world.[2]

Consider what happens, then, when God seeks someone to deliver His provision to people in financial need but person after person refuses to become involved. If that should happen in your case, *even though God said yes to your desperate plea,* today could end with you staring into empty hands.

Try to comprehend for a moment the desperate prayers God is hearing right now. So many prayers for rescue, for milk for the baby, for a few dollars to feed the kids or to keep the lights on. And that's just from the people you and I will see today! Multiply that number by untold millions of pleas from across the globe, and we begin to grasp the larger picture.

In His unfailing compassion, God is constantly search-ing for people who will respond. Every day and all over the world, He sends out a symphony of invitations for people to partner with Heaven to deliver His answer.

But how many will respond? From what people around the world have told me, I'd say only a few.

That's why I believe it's accurate and utterly respectful to say that, when it comes to meeting urgent financial needs, God can appear to be out of funds. (As one busi-nessperson described it, "God is asset rich—He owns it all. But He is cash poor—all His funds are in our hands!") Unless people respond for Him and with Him to needs just like yours, critical needs could go unmet. And that is never what God wants.

The "something or someone" that gets in the way of God's loving provision? It's people. Sometimes it's you or me.

One day my wife and I set out to find a practical way to change that. We wanted to make sure that we weren't obstructing God but rather were partnering faithfully with Him to meet real needs in our world. I must tell you, though, what started out as a new approach to personal giving turned into an eye-opening, life-changing adventure with God.

Every day and all over the world, God sends out a symphony of invitations for people to partner with Heaven.

It all began like this…

What "ready and willing" looks like

Many years ago my wife and I felt that too often we were missing out on the thrill of personal, hands-on, God-directed giving. We gave regularly and joyfully to our church and other worthy causes, and we were certainly blessed to help out family members and others when we could. But increasingly, our giving seemed impersonal, even automatic (and this was in the days before the auto-deduct options on bank accounts). By and large, our giving reflected *our* decisions based on *our* understanding and *our* priorities.

What would happen, Darlene and I wondered, if in addition to our regular giving at church, we could be more purposeful about living in active, daily dependence on God to direct our personal giving?

That way, God could move our funds around where, when, and to whom He wanted. We could serve as His delivery agents. He'd get all the glory, and we'd have front-row seats to one divine provision after another. We needed a practical, God-honoring way to do just that.

Finally a verse in 1 Timothy opened our eyes. The more we prayed about it, the more we saw that this verse might be giving us the answer we'd been looking for.

Paul gives young pastor Timothy a picture of how Christians can invite God into their giving in a big way:

> *Let them do good, that they be rich in good works, ready to give, willing to share.*[3]

Notice especially the words "ready to give, willing to share." They sound like advice you might give a kindergartner on his first day of school. But don't be fooled. These powerhouse words reveal the difference between mere good intentions and life-changing actions.

"Ready and willing" does not, for example, describe a college athlete who merely tells everyone how much he loves to run. Not a chance. Picture the same athlete crouching in the starting blocks, leaning forward, listening intently, ready to launch himself down the track as soon as the starting gun fires. *That* is ready and willing!

Practically speaking, "ready and willing" suggests that all obstacles have been removed beforehand. In other words, the decisions, preparation, and commitment that are required in order for us to act successfully have already been taken care of.

That way, when God signals, we can respond immediately.

The more Darlene and I thought about Paul's advice to be "ready to give, willing to share," the more we understood that our problem might lie not in *what* or *where* we gave but in *how we gave.* What we needed most was to find a way to respond without hesitation whenever and wherever God led.

The God Pocket became the perfect solution.

THE SEVEN STEPS TO YOUR GOD POCKET ADVENTURE

The God Pocket is a tool that anyone can use to meet urgent needs as Heaven directs. The idea is rooted in the Principle of Advance Transfer—you transfer ownership to God of a specific sum *ahead of time* so that when He chooses, He can meet someone else's financial need through you.

Your commitment ahead of time to act allows you to emotionally separate yourself from the money in your God Pocket. You are just the delivery agent, a messenger on a mission. The funds you carry belong to God to do with as He pleases.

> The God Pocket is rooted in the Principle of Advance Transfer—you transfer ownership to God of a specific sum ahead of time so that when He chooses, He can meet someone else's financial need through you.

Now you can relax, because the next move is entirely up to Him.

Here are seven simple but liberating steps that have prepared thousands just like you to make their exciting God Pocket deliveries.

Step 1. Decide.

Decide how much money you are going to place into your God Pocket. The amount you choose to put into your God Pocket isn't nearly as important as deciding to put some in! Five, ten, twenty, two hundred dollars? In my experience, no amount, when devoted to God, is too small or too big.

God knows every person around you who is asking Him to provide or who is just wishing He would. He can and will lead you to the person who would be thrilled with the exact amount you carry.

Step 2. Devote.

Devote that amount of money directly to God. To *devote* something or someone, in the Biblical sense, means you are handing over ownership—in this case to God. You are devoting your funds to God now, in advance, not when you make the actual delivery to the person. These funds are separate from and in addition to what you give to your church or other commitments. These are for God to use at the time and for the person of His choosing.

Devoting a specific amount to God ahead of time means that the normal struggle of parting with it has already been resolved. When the opportunity to deliver the money in your God Pocket presents itself, you won't be thinking about all the things you might have used it for. You're less likely to postpone your response to God's leading and thus miss the opportunity right in front of you.

Physically lift up your cash to Heaven and sincerely pledge: "God, I wholeheartedly devote this money to You. As of this moment, it's no longer mine but Yours. I promise that I will deliver it whenever and wherever and to whomever You choose."

Step 3. Deposit.

Deposit your devoted money into your God Pocket. Your God Pocket can be a small pouch you carry or a specific location in your wallet or purse where you deposit God's money. Increasingly, my wife and I—and many others we know—prefer to use specially produced God Pockets because they improve our effectiveness at the moment of delivery and help us make this an ongoing practice. (More on that later.)

Wherever you place your devoted money, don't let it get confused with other funds. The only money that goes into the God Pocket are funds that have been devoted to God. Never treat them like a cash reserve, even if you forget to bring offering money to church. Remember, what's in your God Pocket no longer belongs to you.

Step 4. Depend.

Depend upon God to lead you to the exact person He has in mind. This step describes the key phase in a God Pocket experience. You are relying on God to do what you cannot do—lead you to the person He wants to bless with the contents of your God Pocket. As you'll see in the pages ahead, He *will* lead you—often in the most surprising ways imaginable.

During this time of dependence, ask God sincerely and often to lead you to the person of His choice. Then go about your day alert to His direction, consciously trusting that when He wants to meet a financial need through you, He will let you know.

How will you recognize God's leading? We'll talk more about that in the next chapter, but for now you can rest assured that some important things about your life have already changed—and all for the better. God is thrilled that you want to partner with Him and share some of your resources with others. From Heaven's perspective, you are a rare and valued partner. You are God's delivery agent—"ready to give, willing to share."

Step 5. Deliver.

Deliver God's funds to the recipient. Everything to this point has been preparation. In this fifth step you move into action. When God nudges you, you reach for your God Pocket and deliver Heaven's provision.

Whether you carry God's money in a designated place in your wallet or purse or in a specially created pouch, an effective delivery occurs in the course of a natural conversation where you give God's provision to the needy person of God's choosing. In chapter 4 we'll explore some simple guidelines for a comfortable and effective delivery. You'll quickly discover that when you partner with God, He can be trusted to work out the details. Why? Because He wants you to deliver His funds to the right person at the right time even more than you do!

Step 6. Declare.

Declare that God is the ultimate Giver who provided this financial gift for them. In this step you transfer the credit. How? You tell the recipient something as simple as, "This money belongs to God, not me. I'm just the delivery person." After all, He arranged the encounter, and the funds belonged to Him—you were just carrying them around! The God Pocket is a showcase not for your generosity and concern but for God's. That's why it's so important that He receives the credit He deserves for lovingly bringing you together with the person He had in mind.

Because God directed you to the precise person at the precise moment, you can rest assured that He also prepared your recipient to receive His provision. In fact, in my experience, both the delivery person *and* the recipient get swept up in a natural outpouring of profound gratitude to God for His mysterious and wonderful provision.

Step 7. Disciple.

Disciple the person by encouraging them to deliver God Pockets too. You won't always be delivering God's money to people who are in a position to give to others. But often you will. Consider the seventh step as an invitation to an opportunity. What I mean is that the God Pocket is a perfect tool to launch other people into an active, daily ministry partnership with God. After all, they've just been surprised by God's presence and provision. They'll likely find the prospect that they could pass along the same unforgettable experience to someone else to be both thrilling and motivating.

Sometimes I will merely ask, "It's obvious that the God Pocket meant a great deal to you. Would you like to be able to deliver your own God Pockets to others just as I did?" I have yet to meet anyone who didn't become excited at the thought.

If you are using a specially created God Pocket, consider gifting them with yours, then briefly share with them the simple process of partnering with God to deliver His money to others in need. Imagine the greater number of lives you will dramatically affect as you share with others

THE 7 DS OF THE GOD POCKET

Step 1 ▪ **Decide** how much money you are going to place into your God Pocket.

Step 2 ▪ **Devote** that amount of money directly to God.

Step 3 ▪ **Deposit** your devoted money into your God Pocket.

Step 4 ▪ **Depend** upon God to lead you to the exact person He has in mind.

Step 5 ▪ **Deliver** God's funds to the recipient calmly and effectively.

Step 6 ▪ **Declare** that God is the ultimate Giver who provided the money.

Step 7 ▪ **Disciple** the person to deliver their own God Pockets to others.

how to use this simple tool to partner with God in meeting urgent needs!

YOUR STORY BEGINS HERE

Do you see it now? Yes, God could drop money from Heaven, just as He could write the Good News across the sky. But His solution is much more personal, intimate, and life changing. He lovingly invites you and me to take His generosity to people in need. What an amazing privilege! And every time we open our God Pocket, all of Heaven cheers us on as yet another discouraged heart is filled to overflowing with God's goodness and care.

In the years Darlene and I have been devoting money in advance to God, we've participated in dozens of miracles of provision. (I call them miracles for one reason, because that's how the recipients invariably describe them.) And as we've shared the practice with others, we've seen individu-

> **Y**es, God could drop money from Heaven, just as He could write the Good News across the sky. But His solution is much more personal, intimate, and life changing.

als, couples, and whole churches step into a great adventure of generosity with Him. As you'll see in the pages ahead, their stories are as varied as the people who experienced them, but each one reveals the presence of a personal, generous, wonder-working God.

In the next chapter you'll begin to recognize the seven steps at work in the stories. In short order the steps will become second nature to you.

You'll also see that every story—yours included—begins when someone tunes in to the symphony of invitations that Heaven sends our way.

Are you ready?

Because right now, one of those invitations is on its way to you.

The God Pocket
He owns it. You carry it. Suddenly, everything changes!

3

Was That a Nudge?

How God leads you to the person He wants
to bless with your God Pocket

Your God Pocket is ready, you have decided to act when
God directs, and you're waiting for His signal.

What should you expect to happen next?

*For Steve, what happened next was an unexpectedly
speedy answer to prayer.* He was at a downtown restaurant
for a birthday celebration—lots of kids and noise. "I wan-
dered outside after I finished eating just to escape the

chaos for a few minutes," recalls Steve. But on his way out the door, Steve told the Lord that what he wanted more than peace and quiet was to deliver his God Pocket to someone in need.

On the sidewalk he struck up a conversation with a well-dressed man. As they chatted, it became apparent to Steve that the man needed to be on the other side of town and couldn't figure out how to get there. "He just opened up to me," says Steve. "Gradually I realized this was a divine arrangement and I should take it seriously."

Even though Steve had no reason to believe the man lacked resources, he found himself asking if the man needed cab fare to get where he needed to be. Steve says, "He looked stunned and said, almost embarrassed, 'Yes! Actually, I do.'" So Steve reached for his devoted money. "When I told him it was from my God Pocket, the guy looked up to the skies and shouted, 'Praise You, Jesus!' Then he gave me a big hug!"

For Jill, what came after waiting for God's signal was a faith-testing plot twist. She felt strongly nudged to deliver funds from her God Pocket to a woman at her church.

Jill didn't know her well, and when she drove up to the woman's house, Jill saw that it was nicer than hers. A lot nicer.

At that moment, she told me, she felt tempted to turn around. Why would God want her to give His money to someone who seemed to be doing so well? Had she made a mistake, misread God's nudge? "But as I was thinking these thoughts," Jill says, "I sensed the Holy Spirit reminding me that things aren't always as they seem. So I got out of my car and proceeded to the door."

Jill discovered that the woman was in dire financial straits. She had been laid off some time ago, had been unable to find new work, and was falling behind in her payments. "It seemed very likely to me that she was going to lose the house," says Jill. To top it off, the woman's son had sickle cell anemia, and the cold weather was aggravating his symptoms. The woman told Jill she needed to buy her son a winter coat but didn't have the money.

"God had sent me directly to her. If I had responded based only on what I could see, I would have missed an opportunity to deliver His provision to the woman and her child. The very next Sunday she and her kids stopped by my Sunday school class because her son wanted to show me his new coat!"

Both stories you've just read highlight an important question: how does God lead you and me so that we can deliver His provision to the right person? After all, in this book we're not just talking about general giving—as important as that is. We're focusing on a special kind of giving, one with a distinct protocol where we prepare in advance so that God can guide us to deliver His provision to a person with a need we couldn't know about otherwise.

> God doesn't leave something this important to chance—it's His money and His heart on the line.

This chapter expands on the fourth step in the God Pocket delivery process: *Depend upon God to lead you to the exact person He has in mind.* You're going to see that God doesn't leave something this important to chance— it's His money and His heart on the line. If you and I are alert and ready to do what God asks, He will lead us to the right person time after time.

DIRECTED BY GOD

Especially when we're newcomers to the God Pocket, we're naturally concerned that we might make a mistake. Will we be able to tell whether it is divine direction or the extra-shot latte talking? We can imagine some pretty awkward scenarios.

But the truth is, human "mistakes" with the God Pocket are rare. Here's why: Your steps of preparation have already removed many obstacles, including indecision, unpreparedness, unbelief, and attachment to the money. Now Heaven is ready to work through you—in your day and with your interests, your aptitudes, and even your inadequacies—to connect you with a person God wants to help.

I'll put it another way:

1. God has *someone exactly* in mind.

2. You have *exactly no one* in mind.

That gives God a lot of room to work. You have surrendered not only what's in your God Pocket but your need to control what happens next. You are now in God's sweet spot, and He's highly motivated to reveal His heart of compassion through you.

Which brings us to the single most important way we find our God Pocket appointments.

THAT INNER PUSH

It is a signal from Heaven I call the *God Nudge.*

A nudge is an inner push that directs us toward a person, a place, or an action. It is a signal from God that unexpectedly focuses our attention on someone, directing us to something God wants done.

In chapter 1 you watched as God nudged Darlene twice—once when she realized that God wanted to encourage Margie, the KFC counter clerk, and again when she realized that God had orchestrated her second meeting with the distraught young wife.

When you decide to follow as God leads you to the person He has in mind, Heaven becomes deeply invested in your success.

In this chapter you saw how nudges directed Steve and Jill to do things that at first seemed unnecessary. But when they acted on Heaven's leading anyway, they discovered what God saw—two people in financial trouble.

What are the common elements in these stories?

- Darlene, Steve, and Jill were going about their lives.
- But they were "ready to give, willing to share." Their God Pocket preparations had already been made.
- They were alert to God's leading.
- And God did lead them. His nudges came as a strong inner tug or an impossible-to-miss coincidence.
- Upon recognizing a God Nudge, each of them reached for his or her God Pocket and passed on God's provision to a person in need.
- And Heaven broke through!

When you decide to follow as God leads you to the person He has in mind, Heaven becomes deeply invested in your success. Some of the most inspiring God Pocket stories I've heard are ones in which God seemed to be guiding His delivery agents through a maze of circumstances...and smiling all the while.

A winding path to "perfect"

This God Nudge story follows a winding path of things that didn't go right—that is, until they ended perfectly—for a guy named Jeff. (I'll highlight what *didn't go right* to show you what I mean.)

Some equipment Jeff uses in his business *stopped working,* so he scheduled a trip Thursday to a city an hour and a half away to get the equipment repaired. Then *unexpected interruptions came up,* and he couldn't make it. Early Friday morning he tried again, this time inviting his son along for company. But when they arrived at the repair facility, *the repairman wasn't there.* They'd have to wait.

And wait they did.

The repair wasn't completed until nearly noon. What a frustration! Says Jeff, "As my son and I headed out of the city toward home, we decided we might as well stop for lunch." But by the time they decided, *they'd already passed the restaurant* they had in mind. Should they just keep driving?

They decided to turn around. At the restaurant they went to the rest room to wash up, but *the facility wasn't working.* More frustration. They waited while a young man took care of the problem.

And at that point Jeff began to wonder if maybe, just maybe, God was up to something. "That young man's attitude in an unpleasant situation was exceptional," recalls Jeff. "It struck a chord with me. But it wasn't until after we had ordered our food that I felt the nudge." Surprised, Jeff looked around for the employee, but *he was nowhere in sight.*

"Okay, God," Jeff prayed, "maybe I didn't really feel a nudge. But if this young man needs a miracle from You, let him come into the dining room so I can talk to him."

Within ten seconds here he came. But instead of coming fully into the dining room, he made a left turn and *exited the building.*

Jeff contemplated his options. By no stretch of the imagination was he expecting to be eating lunch on this day in this city in this restaurant. And speaking of his imagination, had his day of things not going right scrambled his senses?

He decided to try again.

"Okay, God, I still don't know if this was a nudge," he

prayed. "But if it was, let the young man still be in the parking lot, maybe talking on his cell phone, when we're finished eating."

Ten minutes later Jeff and his son left the restaurant. And sure enough, the employee was standing in the parking lot, just getting off a call. Jeff walked over to say hello.

"I told him about the nudge and described my back-and-forth conversation with God regarding him," says Jeff. "Then I told him that I felt we had met for a reason and that God wanted me to give him the money in my God Pocket."

Amazed at what was happening, the young man started spilling his story. He and his mother had recently moved to the city. But for the past few weeks, a medical procedure had left her unable to work. They were trying to make ends meet. He was training to be a manager at a different location of this restaurant chain. Actually, he wasn't supposed to be here today, he told Jeff. He'd just stopped by on an errand.

"Of course I told him that I wasn't supposed to be here today either but that God has an amazing way of working things out," says Jeff. "His eyes began to fill with tears, and he said that he needed to call his mother and tell her about the miracle.

"I told him, 'God sent me here today to let you know that He knows your situation, He loves you, and He sent someone to help.'"

QUALITIES OF A NUDGE

Do you see how God connected Jeff and the young employee? The men thought their day had turned into an obstacle course of frustrations, delays, U-turns, and dead ends. But God was working through each obstacle. He had a plan for Jeff's day. He had a plan for the young employee—and his mother too. When the men finally crossed paths, God clearly nudged Jeff.

And nudged him again.

And again. (I think God was smiling the whole time!)

And the miraculous provision God had in mind was delivered right on time.

Sometimes a God Nudge directs us toward a person in our line of sight. "I suddenly became aware of him sitting there, and I knew something important was up," we might say. Or, "God just opened my heart to her." Other times the person may not be around. We might describe this experience with words like "I felt God leading me toward…" or "Out of nowhere I just knew I had to call Aunt Iris."

Whatever person or need they lead us toward, nudges tend to have certain qualities in common:

A nudge is unexpected and out of context. You might be driving to work or brushing your teeth when it comes: *Go talk to that man* or *Stop here.* A God Nudge rarely comes in the middle of your thoughts about the intended person, place, or event but rather interrupts your thoughts about something else. God wants you to recognize that He's saying, *This thought isn't yours but Mine!*

A nudge is uncomfortable. A God Nudge invites you to do something you may not want to do, such as start a conversation with someone you barely know. We commonly assume that if God is asking us to do something, we should feel great peace in doing it. But the truth is often just the opposite. God's work almost always requires that we stop what we're doing, or would prefer to do, and make His agenda our priority.[1]

A nudge is subtle but clear. God's signal to us will be

clear enough that we will know we received the message. We often wish that He would provide more details. But when information or an explanation is missing, God wants us to exercise faith and act on what we have received.

Confirmation

If you're wondering what to do when you've been nudged, remember that your most important next step is always forward. That's what Jeff did. He asked God to show him if the perceived nudge was for real, *and he continued to move forward in faith, ready and willing to act as God directed.* Similarly, the most wonderful God Pocket experiences I've had are those in which I didn't know until afterward what God was up to.

If you're wondering what to do when you've been nudged, remember that your most important next step is always forward.

But walking by faith doesn't require that we always walk blind. In chapter 8 of my book *You Were Born for This,* I suggest several other signals, in addition to the God Nudge, that I use all the time in ministry. Two important signals can help confirm that a nudge is from Heaven, not your imagination:

A cue is an outward sign of need in another person. People send cues by what they say, how they look, or how they act. Parents, teachers, caring friends, and many kinds of trained professionals watch for cues because they indicate how someone else is feeling. Now that you carry a God Pocket, you're going to be much more attuned to needs around you. A lady at a bus stop is quietly crying. A man is holding a sign asking for money to feed his children. A woman on the treadmill next to you says her life is falling apart.

Did God put them in your path? More to the point, does He have a God Pocket provision in mind for them?

Maybe. But then again, maybe not.

You and I are called to care deeply about others in need, and God can use cues to get our attention. Still, not every sign of need means that God is asking you to deliver His money. That would quickly become impossible. You might, of course, feel drawn to be generous with your own resources—and that could be a very good thing. But as you know by now, that's different from using your God Pocket.

When you see an obvious need, pay closer attention, but don't reach for God's money until you sense His nudge.

A bump is a question intended to surface a hidden need. Like a cue, a bump provides more information that can lead you toward, and will support, a God Nudge. In *The Prayer of Jabez,* I wrote about my favorite bump: "How may I help you?" But there are many others. For instance, we bump a person every time we say, "How's it going?" (We just don't always listen for the answer.)

If you're uncertain about whether you felt a nudge or have the right person, don't hesitate to bump for more information: "You look a little lost. Can I help you?" God won't dock you points because you reached out with a question that would surface an important need. He's delighted that you are proactively searching for the intended recipient of His gift.

Just be sure to apply the same standard for a bump as for a cue. Pay close attention to what your question reveals, but don't reach for God's money until you sense His nudge.

WATCHING FOR THE NUDGE

In the following story, watch how God used a nudge to show me His heart for a person in need. And watch, too, how my question (bump), followed by someone else's description of a need (cue), confirmed that God had brought us together for a God Pocket delivery.

I had flown into Atlanta on another airline and needed a boarding pass on Delta for the last leg home. After walking to my departure gate, I gave the attendant my name and asked if she could print a boarding pass for me. I was early, no one else was around, and we chatted while she tracked down my reservation. Then she paused. "You wouldn't happen to be an author, would you?" she asked.

I smiled and acknowledged that I was. Then... *Was that a nudge?* I wondered. But I wasn't sure.

She leaned forward. "My father died a few months ago," she said quietly. "Your *Prayer of Jabez* book meant so very much to him. He prayed that prayer for the past ten years, and his life really changed. I can't thank you enough."

We still had the counter to ourselves, so I asked about her life. Fifteen years earlier her husband had left her to

GO, TURN, STOP

How we get from here to there, God's way

We locate a God Pocket appointment by receiving and responding to direction from Heaven. This inner prompt or push is called a **nudge**:

- A nudge is an inner push that directs us toward a person, a place, or an action. It is a signal from God that unexpectedly focuses our attention on someone, directing us to something God wants done.

To make sure we give away God's money only when He asks, we don't take action unless we sense this signal from Heaven. But we can use two other ministry signals—a **cue** and a **bump**—to confirm a nudge:

- A cue is an outward sign of need in another person.
- A bump is a question intended to surface a hidden need.

raise five children alone. It had been a struggle, but her kids were growing up into remarkable people. "They're all doing so well in school and at work," she said. "Most importantly, all of them love and serve the Lord. I couldn't be any more thankful."

"What an inspiring example you are!" I told her. "You've really encouraged me." And then a question occurred to me. I meant it as an intentional bump. "This has been a challenging year in the airline industry," I said. "Have you been affected by the downturn?"

With that question her tone changed completely. "I must admit, things have been tough. *Really* tough," she said. "We all took pay cuts, and lately I've been struggling terribly with the bills. Today the pressure feels overwhelming."

As she talked and I watched her expression of concern, I sensed a second, stronger nudge. Truthfully, it was more like a special invitation in flashing letters for me to deliver His provision!

PREPARED TO DELIVER

I'll tell you what happened next at that ticket counter in the following chapter. But now that you realize how dependably God will direct you to the right person, you're ready to make your own God Pocket delivery.

For the rest of your life, you'll remember that God used you—personally, dramatically, and effectively—to reveal Himself to another person. The other person will remember the incident in much the same way.

In fact, the people I've delivered God's provision to have nearly always taken it further. They've called these hand-delivered gifts from God…a miracle.

THE GOD POCKET

He owns it. You carry it. Suddenly, everything changes!

4

AGENTS IN ACTION

Your job description for successful
God Pocket deliveries

Brent's first clue that God might have a delivery for him came at four in the morning in a run-down neighborhood. "Usually when I see something suspicious in the street that early, I stay clear—for my own safety and that of my company's property," he wrote in an e-mail. But that morning things were different.

Brent drives a truck for a grocery-store chain in the Chicago area. When he left his house at 1:00 a.m., he made a decision. You could say he took on a second job. "That morning I let God know I was ready to deliver a God Pocket and I would be paying attention."

Three hours later he was at Seventy-third and Pulaski when he saw a Ford Focus with its flashers on. Instead of driving by, he pulled up next to the car and rolled down the window.

"I saw that there was a lady inside. When I asked what was wrong, she said she was almost out of gas and was afraid of running out. So she'd just pulled over. Then she had realized she didn't have money to buy gas."

As Brent listened, he remembered what he had said to God when he left the house. He got out of his truck and reached for his God Pocket.

After explaining to the motorist that the funds were God's, not his, he gave her money for fuel. Then for some reason he felt he should ask if she knew the Lord. "Yes, I do!" she said. "Jesus Christ is my Savior. I have been sitting here praying that He would keep me safe—and He sent you! Now I know that I am safe!"

Brent told her how *he* had prayed that very morning that God would send him to a person who needed something from God. They both agreed—she was the person!

After he helped her find the nearest all-night gas station, they parted. "I drove away shaking my head in wonder and amazement," Brent wrote. "Glory to the Lord! And there's more. After work that morning I went to Macy's department store because some items my wife and I had recently purchased were on sale. The amount the store credited back to my account was the exact amount I had given the lady in the car."

In this chapter I want you to see the God Pocket in action. I'll help you understand in practical terms what to expect, how to make a God Pocket delivery, and what to say. I want to be as helpful as possible because I'm describing something I hope will be of great interest to you.

Your new job description.

PROFILE OF A DELIVERY AGENT

I call people who carry God Pocket money to give to those in need "Delivery Agents." A delivery person, as you well know, might bring a package to your house or business. Delivery people understand that what matters to you is not who brought the package but what's in it. Their job is to get you and your package together.

When you and I are delivery agents for God, we take on the same role. What really matters is that the package—what's in our God Pockets—moves from our hands into the hands of the person God desires to have it. Our part is simply to follow God's directions (we saw in the previous chapter how that happens), make the human connection, and deliver the goods.

In my experience, God's delivery agents are refreshingly ordinary folks. They aren't spiritual giants, gifted speakers, brilliant Bible scholars, or even unusually nice. Did I mention remarkably holy? They're not that either. Instead, they are everyday men, women, teenagers, and children who love God, care about others, and have discovered the rewards of using God's money to reveal His heart to hurting people.

Who qualifies for the job? Anyone who sincerely desires to partner with God, knowing that the plan is all God's and therefore the credit is all God's too.

Take Brent. His story, like the others you've encountered, reveals the profile of a delivery agent. For example:

He's just who he is. In his case it's Brent, grocery-truck driver. Yet he believes that God can show up just as certainly in his day as in anyone else's.

He has experienced a shift in perspective. He understands now that God deeply desires to pour out His goodness *through him* to others—not just once, but often. In fact, this event of "God showing up through Brent" could happen today. That's why…

He always carries funds in his God Pocket. Brent has devoted funds to God to do with as He wishes. Brent carries God's cash with him in case God directs him to give His provision to someone, which could happen at any time. And if He does…

He has made a commitment to act. Before he left the house at 1:00 a.m., Brent told God that all day he would be ready and willing to make a delivery when the nudge came.

He keeps his eyes open. He knows God is invisibly at work in every circumstance. And he knows that an effective delivery agent needs to be awake to and aware of seemingly ordinary things, such as a car pulled over with its flashers on.

God's delivery agents are refreshingly ordinary folks. They aren't spiritual giants, gifted speakers, brilliant Bible scholars, or even unusually nice.

He takes a risk for God. When the nudge came, he didn't drive by. Even though he doesn't typically stop in dangerous neighborhoods in the middle of the night in his company truck, he pulled over. He discovered that he had made his connection—with a frightened woman in trouble.

He reaches for his God Pocket. In just moments the woman has money for fuel. Fear gone. Problem solved. And Brent is a hero?

Oh not at all. Because right away...

He transfers the credit to God. Brent let her know that the money belonged to God, not him. When they discovered that God had brought them together in answer to *both* their prayers, they celebrated His loving-kindness.

Does Brent's profile help bring the process of delivering a God Pocket miracle into sharper focus for you? I hope so. By now, a pattern for deliveries should be emerging for you. Let me show you how the familiar pattern reveals itself again in one of my favorite God Pocket encounters.

It took me by surprise in a department store in the Rocky Mountains.

"Somebody sent me"

I had been searching the display case for a much-needed new watch when I became aware of another shopper at the same counter. She had been trying on a particular watch for some time, apparently trying to talk herself into buying it.

"That is a beautiful watch," I said. "It looks like it was made for you!" The turquoise trim on the watch matched her Native American attire perfectly.

"You really think so?" she replied.

"I do. Why don't you get it?"

She said, "Oh, I could never afford this watch."

"That's too bad," I said. "You might not find a watch like that one again."

She said, "I know," but gently set the watch back down on the counter. That's when I received an unexpected but distinct God Nudge. *Oh,* I thought to myself. *Her.* I was taken by surprise. *A turquoise watch? Now?* But the signal was unmistakable.

I caught her eye. "Ma'am, it's not hard to see you would really love that watch. May I have the privilege of buying it for you?"

"What?"

"Wouldn't you like the watch?"

"Yes, very much! But you can't buy it for me!"

"No, I can't," I said. "But a special Friend of mine instructed me to carry around some of His funds. He asked me to keep my eye out for a person I think He would really want to help with His money. When I find that person, I'm supposed to use it on His behalf. My Friend would definitely want you to have this watch."

"Really?" she said, trying to process what she had just heard.

"Oh yes. It's true. He'd really enjoy buying it for you." I motioned to the salesclerk for assistance.

"Oh my goodness!" she said. She stared at the watch, then at me. Then she said, almost to herself, "I had lost all confidence in mankind."

That's when I really noticed her countenance for the first time. Her face was heavily lined and bore an expression of deep sadness. I decided to take another step of faith. I said, "You have really been hurt, haven't you? You've been wounded many times."

"Yes, I have." Her eyes began to tear up.

"Well, Someone who knows about your wounds sent

me all the way from Atlanta to Colorado because He wants you to know that He deeply cares about you." I paused. "Might you know who that is?"

A light seemed to click on for her. "It's God, isn't it?"

"He does love you, doesn't He?" I said quietly.

She was brushing away tears as I made the purchase with my God Pocket funds and handed her the watch.

She said, almost to herself, "I had lost all confidence in mankind."

"Jesus knew sorrow more than anyone you'll ever meet,"[1] I said. "Every time you look at this watch, remember that God loves you and He wants your heart not only to be healed but to sing with joy!"

As I walked out of that store, my heart was singing too.

THREE STARTER QUESTIONS

What I enjoy most about delivering a God Pocket is watching how God uses it to open a person's heart to His love. Money has great power. And there's something about a sudden, generous gift—and from God, no less—that breaks through routine and resistance and reaches deeply into a person's emotions. It didn't take much to convince the woman who had just received a stunning, turquoise-accented gift from her loving Father that He had never stopped caring for her.

You'll quickly find that a God Pocket delivery opens the door to caring conversations of many kinds. That's why I encourage you to be alert to a person's underlying need and to be ready for a conversation that might follow naturally. After all, you have been uniquely prepared to be God's representative at that moment.

Now, to help you get started, I want to respond to three questions that tend to come up with newer delivery agents.

Once I've found my appointment, how do I start the conversation? What do I say?

Hopefully, you've seen a pattern to the God Pocket conversations in this book. No genius required! A typical delivery conversation proceeds in three easy-to-remember steps:

1. Report your nudge. "For some reason you caught my attention."

2. Describe your mission. "This God Pocket money belongs to God. I'm just carrying it around for Him." Or, "I've been carrying this around for God until He tells me whom to give it to."

3. Make your delivery. "I think He wants me to give it to you."

I feel awkward handing money to someone I've just met. Is there an advantage to giving away a God Pocket with the funds in it versus just delivering the money?

Many people have found that using a specially designed pouch with the devoted funds in it significantly eases the God Pocket delivery. You're not fishing around in your wallet or purse—that might suggest to the recipient that you're giving them *your* money. And you're not openly handing over cash, which in some social situations can be awkward. (To learn more about pouches you can order or make, see the resource page at the back of this book or visit www.TheGodPocket.com.)

I closed chapter 3 with a story of how I followed a nudge (confirmed by a cue and a bump) to find a God Pocket appointment at an airport departure gate. Now I'll tell the rest of the story. Watch how giving away a God Pocket with the funds in it helps draw the conversation naturally toward the Lord and His goodness.

Remember, the airport worker was a single mother of five who had just revealed her financial struggles. While she was doing so, God nudged me a second time. Here's what happened next:

I took out my leather God Pocket and laid it on my open palm. "Have you ever seen one of these before?" I asked her, smiling.

She peered at it. "No. I can't say that I have."

"It's for you," I said and held it out.

"For me?"

"Yes, I believe we were brought together today because God knows your struggles. Why not see what's inside?"

She unsnapped the flap, then saw the bills. "Why, I can't take this from you!" she exclaimed.

"Oh, but it's not my money!" I said. "Turn it over and read what it says."

On the other side she read the words *The God Pocket* embossed in bold letters. As she did, her expression softened. She put a hand to the side of her face in amazement. "It's a miracle," she whispered.

"What you have there is God's money," I continued. "I've just been carrying it around for Him, waiting to find the person He wanted to touch today. And there's no doubt—it's you!"

What's the best way to give God the credit?

When you deliver God's money, you've already set the stage for Him to receive the glory. The last thing people expect is a gift of money, much less money from God! When out of nowhere He interrupts their day with a God Pocket, they suddenly hold proof that He cares, that their life has purpose.

Transferring credit to God happens naturally when you follow these three steps:

1. Share the joy. "I'm really happy for you too!"
2. Transfer the credit. "God arranged all this for you. Isn't He amazing?"
3. Affirm God's character. "God wants you to know He really cares about you."

Notice that you're keeping the focus on the event God has arranged, not on you. And that probably won't be hard. As a delivery agent told me, "People who receive a God Pocket aren't thinking of you. They are thinking about what has just happened to them. And they're ready to conquer the world!"

THE JOY FACTOR

Which brings me to my favorite God Pocket–related word. When you leave your house with your God Pocket, get ready for *joy*. I know Brent would agree. He came away from his God Pocket delivery that early morning overwhelmed with joy and gratitude.

And why expect anything less? Pure joy springing up is the indisputable proof of God's presence.[2]

> **When you leave your house with your God Pocket, get ready for joy.**

I guarantee you'll see joy in the person to whom you deliver your first God Pocket. It happened right away to Ross and his wife. They delivered their God Pocket funds to a waitress named Sara. Soon afterward, they received the following e-mail:

Hi, this is Sara, your food server who waited on you and your wife last Friday. I want to thank you two so very much for your kind gift. I have never in my ten years of serving tables been given anything like that. When I saw the money, I got chills and wanted to cry.

The day prior, I was talking to my husband about these difficult economic times and how we are struggling. We had received an unexpected bill in the mail for medical services of over two hundred dollars. But God meant for us to meet. This was His way of letting me know that things are going to be okay.

I feel so special that you and your wife gave me this gift. It has been a wonderful experience and something I have shared with family and friends. They, too, believe it is incredible and something out of a Hallmark movie, not something that happens to ordinary people like me. Thank you so much.

Notice how Sara described her experience with words like "I feel so special," "wonderful," "incredible," and "something out of a Hallmark movie." She had just received a personal message from God—a message she may have been waiting all her life to hear.

And then there's the delight that delivery agents themselves experience.

When Tommy had a God Pocket encounter with a woman in a mall in Georgia who needed help buying an orthopedic boot, her need—fifty dollars—matched what he had in his Pocket exactly. She came away with

WHAT TO DO, WHAT TO SAY

A checklist for delivery agents

Before a God Pocket delivery...

- Make your decision. "God, I'm ready to give, willing to share."
- Prepare your God Pocket. "This belongs to You, God. I'm just carrying it for You today."
- Stay alert to a God Nudge. "Help me recognize Your leading."

During a God Pocket delivery...

- Report your nudge. "For some reason you caught my attention."

a provision and an "out of the blue" personal message that God cared. Tommy? He came away with something too.

"I told God I would deliver a miracle wherever He wanted me to," Tommy said. "And He led me right to the section of the mall where she was. I was just the delivery

- Describe your mission. "This belongs to God. I'm just carrying it around for Him."
- Make your delivery. "I think He wants me to give it to you."

After a God Pocket delivery...
- Share the joy. "I'm really happy too!"
- Transfer the credit. "God arranged this for us. Isn't He amazing?"
- Affirm God's character. "God wants you to know He really loves you."

man, but I think the best gift may have been for me. God is faithful! God is awesome!"

When Philippe responded to a God Nudge to help a stranger on a commuter-train platform in Massachusetts, what the recipient got was the money he desperately needed for a train ticket. "He was so shocked he couldn't even move at first!" wrote Philippe. "And he kept telling me, 'Thank you!'"

I have never felt like this in my life.

But what impressed Philippe even more was his own reaction. "I knew God had sent me to bring a smile to the face of someone I didn't know. I felt very, very, very good! I have never felt like this in my life. I know it was God who led me there. Now every day I ask God to send me to someone else in need."

WHY DO YOU SUPPOSE…

Why do you suppose God pours so much happiness into the lives of His delivery agents? Is it because we share His heart for the poor and needy? Is it because when we venture into our days "ready to give, willing to share," we are the cheerful givers He so loves? Is it because we are intent on bringing Him the credit and good name He deserves?

Any one of these reasons would easily explain the joy factor of the God Pocket. But in the next chapter I will show you two more.

The first suggests just how much God desires that we are able, in practical terms, to keep refilling our God Pocket time after time—so we can always be "ready to give."

And the second reveals the truly staggering ways God promises to bless us for partnering with Him—not just now, but far into our future.

THE GOD POCKET
He owns it. You carry it. Suddenly, everything changes!

5

The Mystery of Multiplying

God's surprising plan to replenish
your resources when you give

I wonder if you caught it—the "and there's more" part to Brent's story in the previous chapter.

Right when you figured his delivery story was over, the story kept going. After his shift, Brent went to Macy's because some items he and his wife had recently purchased had gone on sale. Here are Brent's own words:

"The amount the store credited back to my account was the exact amount I had given the lady in the car."

Do you find that intriguing?

Truth is, many God Pocket partners I've talked to have had similar experiences. I certainly have. And it keeps happening—what looks to us like God finding creative ways to give us back the money we give away.

Could it really be the case, or are we just imagining things? After all, you and I don't say yes to the God Pocket because we want or expect anything back. The act of giving is our response in obedience to God's nudge, and the joy we experience as a result is reward enough.

But does God see it that way? Is it possible that, while you and I are adding and subtracting, God is busy multiplying?

How God sees and responds to our giving matters a lot, especially if we want to serve Him often and generously with our God Pockets. Sooner or later, you'll wonder, as I have, if you will be able to find more funds for more deliveries. And you will want to know if God will ensure that you can.

That's what I want to explore in this chapter. You see, if God's plan for our giving also includes resupplying the giver, then you and I can proceed very differently indeed. For example, it will directly affect how likely we are to practice the Principle of Advance Transfer as a lifestyle. It will also determine whether we reach for our God Pocket cautiously—perhaps even anxiously—or with confidence and anticipation.

Fortunately, the truth you're about to discover is better news than most people have ever imagined. In fact, I believe that once you see what your Heavenly Father has in store for you, you'll never again

> **I**s it possible that, while you and I are adding and subtracting, God is busy multiplying?

underestimate His trustworthiness, His generous intent on your behalf, or His loving delight in you as His servant.

LENDING TO THE LORD

Let's go back to your God Pocket. Whether yours is a dedicated location in your wallet or purse or a specially designed God Pocket, I want to show you what is actually happening from God's point of view when you slip in some devoted money. I think you'll find the discovery nothing less than stunning.

A little-known verse in the Old Testament provides an important clue to what we could call the Banking System of Heaven:

> *He who has pity* [acts of compassion] *on the poor lends to the LORD.*[1]

The shock here is the word *lends.* Could Scripture be saying that Heaven views our God Pocket delivery not only as *a donation to the person* but also as *a loan to God*?

Now that you know the primary way God gets funds to people in need (by partnering with people), you can see why He so appreciates eager delivery agents. But this verse is about more than appreciation. It seems to quantify God's response in financial terms. With your God Pocket, what you wholeheartedly, with no strings attached, give to Him *as a gift,* He holds in trust for you *as a loan.*

But a loan is a temporary transfer. We usually expect it to be returned. Could the Bible be saying that when we slip something into our God Pockets and give it away to someone in need, God actually plans to restore those funds to us?

For an answer, look with me at the second part of that same verse.

And He [God] *will pay back what he* [the delivery agent] *has given* [to the person in need].[2]

The Bible is not using the word *lends* accidentally but with utter seriousness. God declares that He "will pay back" what you give to a person in need. The words "will pay back" literally mean "will make whole, restore, make compensation, make good." They leave no doubt that God Himself will surely restore to you what you have given.

Are you open to what God reveals about Himself, even if what He reveals doesn't meet your expectations? The fact is, Heaven's Banking System is God's plan and promise. That means it is at work for you whether you believe it or not, have trouble accepting it or not—even whether you have ever heard of it or not!

> **W**hat you wholeheartedly, with no strings attached, give to God as a gift, He holds in trust for you as a loan.

By now you might be wondering what could explain God's motivation to repay those who give. After all, the Bible more than once *commands* us to give to those in need. And when it comes to our God Pocket, we give out of love and gratitude to God. We give because we *want* to give!

But as you're discovering, our Father sees things from a much grander perspective than we do. To illustrate why I believe God is highly motivated to pay back those who give, I'll share a story about a little boy who begged his mom to let him give away her money.

"WHAT MOM WOULDN'T LOVE THAT?"

Our friend Heather was a single mom on food stamps, and one day she took her son Nathan with her to the local super-discount grocery mart. She hated shopping there—it was a dirty, gloomy place with boxes of canned food piled high. But the family couldn't afford to shop at a better grocery store. Nathan, a high-energy six-year-old tow-head, didn't seem to mind the place at all, though. In nearly every aisle, he piped up about something else he really, really—"Oh please, Mommy!"—had to have.

When they got back to the car with their bags, a man carrying a squeegee and a bucket of soapy water walked up and asked if he could wash their windows. "I was annoyed, and I just wanted to get home," Heather recalls. "I kept saying, 'No thank you. Not today. No thank you.' I didn't even make eye contact with the man as I got Nathan and the bags into the car."

But on the way home Nathan seemed worried. Finally he asked his mom to explain what the man in the parking lot had wanted.

"He wanted to clean our car windows," Heather told him. "But really he just wanted money."

"Why? Was he poor?"

"Probably," said Heather. "He doesn't have a real job, I guess."

"But our windows *are* dirty!" Nathan protested. And they were—streaks on the outside, kid prints and dog prints on the inside. Their car sure could have used a wash, Heather admitted.

"So why couldn't you just let him, Mom?" Nathan insisted. He was growing tearful.

Heather tried to explain. "Honey, we're having such a

hard time right now. We don't have money to give away. We're poor too!"

But the more she tried to explain, the more upset Nathan became. By the time they got home, he was begging his mom to give him a chore so he could earn two dollars to give to the man.

"Finally it hit me," says Heather. "My son was brokenhearted, not because he didn't get what he asked for at the store, which was plenty, but because he was thinking about giving to someone else. Which was a good thing—a great thing. What mom wouldn't love that? And *of course* we had a couple of dollars!"

She made a decision. The two climbed into the car and drove back to the discount mart so the man could wash their windows. While the man and his squeegee did their magic, Heather looked over at Nathan in the passenger seat. There he sat, radiating an enormous, gaptoothed grin. In his hands he gripped some crumpled dollars, ready to give to the man the instant he was done.

"I'll never forget that moment," Heather recalls. "I was so proud of him. It made me want to give Nathan a thousand dollars and send him out into the world in search of men with squeegees."

THE PRINCIPLE OF REPLENISHMENT

Wouldn't you have searched high and low for dollars for your child if you had been the parent in that story?

To me, little Nathan's enthusiasm to meet a need and his mother's delight in making a provision possible illustrate what this chapter is about. Nathan wanted to get so he could give. Why wouldn't God, who is more generous than all the mothers in the world put together, want to generously give to His children when *we* want to give?

You've already seen it at work in a number of God Pocket stories. I call it the Principle of Replenishment: when you give, God gives back. It's that simple.

Proverbs 19:17 clearly lays out God's cause-and-effect principle of giving to those in need. It is telling us, "This is how life usually works—when you give, you will also receive." Mind you, what the text is pointing out is a general principle (such as "It pays to be honest") rather than a specific promise ("I will never leave you"). The Bible teaches many such principles—for example, humility comes before honor, hard work brings a profit, and through the fear of the Lord a man avoids evil.[3] These are reliable, God-blessed rules for living wisely and well in our world.

A divinely designed general principle points out the best way to proceed based on what is right or what usually happens. It doesn't, however, guarantee that every time you give a dollar, you'll get exactly a dollar back or that every time you are humble, you will be immediately honored.

Do you see the difference?

The Principle of Replenishment is described in numerous other places in Scripture. For example, "A generous man will prosper; he who refreshes others will himself be refreshed." And "A generous man will himself be blessed, for he shares his food with the poor."[4]

You might be wondering what "will prosper" and "will...be blessed" look like in real life. The answer is that God refreshes the resources of His delivery agents materially—you give money; you receive money back. (That happened to Brent.) But He often does so in additional, equally important ways—you give money; often you also get back an experience you wouldn't trade for ten times the money.

A closer look at the phrases "will prosper" and "will... be blessed" reveals another important insight. They show us who takes charge of giving back. To frame it as a question: "When I give, am I responsible to find more funds, or will God in His own way and in His own time replenish them for me?"

The answer is right in the verses. Both "will prosper" and "will…be blessed" are passive verbs, meaning the action happens *to* you. When you have taken the action step of having compassion on the poor or being generous, you don't have to do anything extra to prosper or be blessed. Why not? Because, as both verbs demonstrate, you now become the recipient, and God becomes the acting agent. And He will act to make sure you will prosper and be blessed.

Which brings us to a very practical, very exciting reason that God chooses to replenish your God Pocket. He has found you to be a faithful giving partner, and He wants to replenish your resources *so that you can give more.*

This principle is so important to God that He expands on this remarkable truth in two entire chapters in the New Testament, 2 Corinthians 8–9. For example, in chapter 9 Paul uses the picture of a farmer sowing seed to explain how replenishment works:

<u>He who sows bountifully will also reap bountifully</u>.
So let each one give as he purposes in his heart, not
grudgingly or of necessity; for God loves a cheerful
giver. And God is able to make all grace abound
toward you, that you, <u>always having all sufficiency</u>
<u>in all things, may have an abundance for every good</u>
<u>work</u>.[5]

If you read the text carefully, you'll note the reason the
Bible gives for God replenishing funds. To make you rich?
You won't find that teaching in any verse in this passage!
Instead, you'll find a single recurring truth. God gives
funds back so that you and I may have *abundance for a*
reason.

And what is that reason?

It is "abundance for every good work." And in this passage Paul links "abundance for every good work" to a single activity—giving to others in need. When you devote
funds to God so that He can meet urgent needs through
you, you are sowing bountifully according to God's priorities, not yours. That means He has every reason to give
back to you what you gave away cheerfully to Him.

By now you might want to ask a personal question: "Bruce, are you telling me—based on the Bible and your life—that this is what I can expect to experience when I put the God Pocket to work in my life? Giving to others and then receiving from God so that I can give again?"

Let me pass along some encouragement. One day I got to wondering if God had ever clearly nudged Darlene or me to give to a person or a group when, due to a lack of finances, we were *not* able to complete the good work. I decided to put the question to Darlene too. As we talked about it, we realized that neither of us could remember that happening. Not even once. In other words, we give testimony that God keeps His promises. When He nudges you to astonish a needy person with His gracious provision, He will make sure that you can. It's your unique good work for Him, after all. And He will make sure you have all sufficiency—abundance, actually—to accomplish it for Him.

But just because God's plan for our giving is good and generous and trustworthy, that doesn't mean it is entirely predictable. I, for one, have experienced the Principle of Replenishment in some very surprising ways.

MY FAVORITE PEN

This story begins and ends with a pen—a Montblanc fountain pen, to be exact. I'm rarely without mine. I tell people it's because I do so much writing longhand. But, honestly, I just love the feel of an old-fashioned, beautifully crafted writing instrument.

One day many years ago I found myself in an appliance store about to sign the purchase documents for a new refrigerator when God nudged me about my highly treasured pen. Here's how it happened:

Darlene and I had decided that whenever we received an unexpected major blessing from the Lord, we would set aside a portion for what we called our thank offerings. Then we would depend upon Him to lead us to a person He wanted us to give it to in His name.

One spring after some funds had come in, our refrigerator stopped working. When the repairman said it wasn't worth fixing, we reluctantly headed down to the appliance store. On the way I said to Darlene, "God hasn't led us to give away our thank offering yet."

At the appliance store the salesman helped Darlene

pick out a new refrigerator. When it came time to pay, he suggested we take advantage of a no-interest special offer if we paid off the appliance in a year. We said that sounded good, and he set about drawing up the paperwork. As we chatted, we discovered he was from west Africa and was working part-time to put himself through school.

As I prepared to sign the papers, I pulled out my Montblanc.

"What a beautiful pen!" the salesman exclaimed. "I have always admired this type of pen! *C'est très magnifique!* Before I return to Côte d'Ivoire, it is my plan to purchase one."

Right then God nudged me. He said, *Give him your Montblanc.*

Fortunately, I was ready. I said to God, *Yes, Lord. I'll give him money from my thank offering. That way he can buy his own pen.*

But the still, small voice was insistent. *Give him your pen.* Clearly the test was about God's giving priorities, not mine. While the salesman shuffled papers, I struggled.

Finally, as I signed on the last dotted line, I said to the man, "Sir, I thought this was my Montblanc pen. But now

I see that it is yours! As we have been visiting, God has been asking me to deliver it to you. So here it is." And I handed him the pen.

He was shocked and delighted. Speechless, really. And when I told him how attached I had become to his pen, we all laughed.

But God's lesson wasn't over. A number of months later I was speaking in California for my friend Pastor David Jeremiah. My subject was consecration. Consecration is when God asks us, not just to give, but to give something that's precious to us—something we don't want to give. In consecration, God is testing our loyalty. To illustrate, I told the audience the story of the Montblanc pen.

Everyone had a good laugh about it. Most of all, Heaven did, because unbeknownst to me, the story was still unfolding.

Months later I was walking down the crowded aisles of an international publishing convention when I heard someone call my name. It was well-known author Tim LaHaye. After we exchanged greetings, Dr. LaHaye told me that David Jeremiah had sent him a recording of my sermon.

"What sermon?" I asked.

"The one about the Montblanc pen," he said. "And you'll never guess what happened. As I was listening to your sermon, God nudged me. More like a shove, really. The message was, *When you see Bruce Wilkinson, give him your Montblanc pen.*"

He reached into his suit pocket and pulled out an old-fashioned, beautifully crafted Montblanc pen. How we laughed! Two men standing in the middle of a busy convention floor, happily astonished at God's plan to resupply us for every good work.

Do you see the Principle of Replenishment at work in my story?

God's replenishment becomes most apparent in our lives when we gladly embrace our role as partners with Heaven to share God's goodness with our world. And our hope in His goodness is never misplaced.

Once you realize how many people in our world are in desperate need and how few are volunteering to partner with God to meet those needs, God's plan and promise for abundance make total sense.

Listen again to His passionate commitment to your

giving. Take in the breadth and depth of His replenishment. Revel in His heart for you, His highly cherished delivery agent:

> *I am able to make <u>all</u> grace abound in your life*
> *so that you will <u>always</u>*
> *have <u>all sufficiency</u>*
> *in <u>all things</u> so that you*
> *will have <u>an abundance</u>*
> *for <u>every</u> good work!*[6]

A GLIMPSE INTO FOREVER

God's plan to replenish our resources as we give with Him is far beyond anything we could have imagined. It's abundance of the most amazing kind! Wouldn't you agree?

And yet, my friend, the Principle of Replenishment is just the beginning of our Father's generous plans for us. There's an even more significant dimension to how God pays us back. It's such a grand truth that it deserves its own book, but the essential principle is this:

When we give to God, He not only resupplies us on earth; *He also repays us in eternity.*[7]

Think of it as the Promise of Repayment. Jesus spoke of it many times.[8] In the gospel of Luke, for example, Jesus gives advice to a dinner host on how to get the most in return for his generosity:

> *When you give a feast, invite the poor, the maimed, the lame, the blind. And <u>you will be blessed</u>, because they cannot repay you; for <u>you shall be repaid at the resurrection of the just</u>.*[9]

What was most shocking for His audience was the *timing* of repayment. You see, they understood the blessing of replenishment on earth—that principle is taught all through the Old Testament. But Jesus was revealing something entirely new. The blessing of repayment by God will not only occur while we are on earth but will continue in eternity "at the resurrection of the just."

The apostle Paul, too, makes a direct connection between our giving on earth and our receiving in Heaven. In fact, he does so in the very text from 1 Timothy that led

Darlene and me to our idea for the God Pocket. As you remember, Paul begins by saying, "Let them do good, that they be rich in good works, ready to give, willing to share…" Look now at how he completes the thought:

> …*storing up for themselves a good foundation for the time to come, that they may lay hold on eternal life.*[10]

Do you see the exponential dimension of partnering with God in your giving on earth? He repays us on earth for our giving so that we can repeatedly have the joy of revealing His loving heart to the world. How? By giving again and again. And He pays us back again in Heaven, where our earthly giving becomes part of our eternal reward. That's why the apostle Paul can say that what you and I give here is stored up as "a good foundation" for our life with Christ in Heaven!

God cares more about giving to those in need than you can ever imagine. Even when we give with no thought of Heaven, even when we give without grasping the eternal implications of our giving—even then God cares so much that He promises to pay us back in full where and when it matters most.

At the beginning of this chapter, we set out to discover how God sees and responds to our decision to be "ready to give, willing to share." I hope you have caught a glimpse of how your God Pocket can open up Heaven's blessings for you and for those God touches through you. In addition to the natural blessings you receive when you give to a person in need, and in addition to God's commitment to supply all your needs[11] so that you can give yet more, God will pay you back fully and finally in Heaven— the only place where your treasure will last forever.[12]

> **W**hat you give here is stored up as "a good foundation" for your life with Christ in Heaven!

LIVING WITH GROWING CONFIDENCE

I pray that what you've read here plants in you the growing confidence in God's abundance that Paul wrote about. Who would have imagined that every time you open your God Pocket, you're not only asking God to reveal His surprising, overflowing, unending goodness to someone in need, but you're also inviting Him to reveal the same to you?

Now that you understand God's plan to multiply your giving through replenishment and repayment, it only makes sense to consider radically expanding your God Pocket partnership.

In the next chapter, you'll meet individuals, couples, families, and churches who are doing just that.

THE GOD POCKET

He owns it. You carry it. Suddenly, everything changes!

6

THE GENEROSITY CONSPIRACY

Stories of God's "little people" who are
reaching for very big things

This might be the most important sentence in the whole book: God wants to partner with you in a conspiracy to reveal Himself to the world.

You've seen evidence in story after story that the people who will come into your life and mine today are hungry for God. Starving even. They want to believe that He notices them. They want to *know* that He cares about them as human beings with names and faces and that He just might—hope against hope—be at work in the details of their lives. Yet these days more than ever, people live in doubt about what they hunger for most.

That's why when I asked at the beginning, "What if you could take a little something out of your pocket today that would make God visible?" I was utterly serious.

Already, people of all ages are using the God Pocket as a simple but powerful tool to reveal God's beauty and goodness to the world. Will you join us? It is our prayer that the God Pocket movement will spread throughout the world the way the prayer of Jabez did. We believe that God wants to put a face on giving—and the face He has in mind is not yours or mine but His.

If you think about it, most of our charity giving these days is delegated to institutions—to a church, for example, or to distant organizations or ministries. Our donations can move from one account to another automatically, no human touch required. You hit a key on your laptop. *Click.* Someone somewhere gets blessed.

Don't misunderstand what I'm saying here. Stewarding our resources and giving to the Lord's work *by what-*

ever means is our privilege, duty, and sincere joy as believers. Nothing about the God Pocket is meant to replace your regular giving to your local church. (In fact, most people I've met who practice the God Pocket become more enthusiastic givers through their local churches—and with more funds to give.)

But when we *only* give indirectly and on a schedule, we're not prepared to partner personally with God to meet urgent needs in the moment. We lose eye contact with the person standing right next to us. We stop living in the thrilling, daily expectation that God

> God wants to put a face on giving— and the face He has in mind is not yours or mine but His.

is ready to use us to reveal His amazing, steadfast goodness around the next corner, at the next coffee shop, or in the next checkout line.

The God Pocket changes all that. We walk into our busy lives as God's messengers, carrying His money, wide awake to His leading. Our simple commitment—carried secretly, delivered openly—changes almost everything about our day.

It has the potential to change us too.

I've noticed a remarkable transformation that comes over people after they've had a God Pocket experience or two. Their Pocket—wherever they carry it—becomes an everyday accessory. They look for creative, personalized ways to give. They begin to grow what goes into their God Pocket, sometimes by a lot.

And then the God Pocket itself begins to grow, and grow some more. Pretty soon their Pocket is as wide and tall and spacious as their wonderful new life.

I call these kindred spirits God Pocket Partners, and in this chapter I want you to imagine your life as one of them. I want to open the window just a crack and show you an amazing future that could be yours.

In their future one young couple saw a miracle waiting to happen, and to them it looked exactly like an electric blue Ford Explorer.

GIVING DIFFERENTLY

Reggie and Skye didn't need their older Ford Explorer anymore, but they couldn't quite bring themselves to sell it either. "There was nothing wrong with it," says Reggie. "A great car—killer sound system, lots of room, perfect for someone. For some reason, though, it just sat in our driveway."

One day they got the message. They were supposed to put their electric blue SUV—all two tons of it—into their God Pocket and let God do what He wanted with it. So that's what they did.

For a month or two, nothing happened. The Ford sat in the driveway while Reggie and Skye second-guessed their nudge-reading skills. They wondered if maybe God didn't think much of SUVs.

Then, in midsummer, a stranger named Howard came to their door looking for yard work. He was pushing a beat-up lawn mower and carrying a can of gas and a few hand tools. Reggie put Howard to work outside.

"He was sweating up a storm, doing a great job," says Reggie. "When he was done, I took the payment and a couple of cold sodas out back. We were sitting on the steps, making small talk, when I asked how he got his equipment around. 'Oh, I just walk it to neighborhoods like this,' he said. 'Takes me awhile, but it works out fine.'"

That's when Reggie noticed right over Howard's shoulder something large and bright blue. As Reggie tells it, God had plunked the Ford down in the middle of their conversation so he couldn't possibly miss the nudge. You can guess what happened next.

"Howard," Reggie said with a big grin, "God brought you to my house for a reason today! I'm sure of it. See that SUV right over there?"

What besides cash could you put—literally or symbolically—into your God Pocket?

Reggie still remembers standing in front of his house, listening to Howard drive away as the new owner of a Ford Explorer, shouting, "Praise You, Jesus! Praise You, Lord!" all the way down the street.

What about you? What besides cash could you put—literally or symbolically—into your God Pocket? I know a business couple who put a time-share condo into their God Pocket, a group of students who put whole Saturdays of free labor into theirs.

The principles of *giving differently* are the same: You transfer something of value in advance to God's ownership, being sensitive to His leading about what that something should be. You prepare to deliver it personally when, where, and to whom God directs. Then you stay alert, ready at any time for His nudge.

Giving more

Many have found that, once they experience the deep, personal fulfillment of giving with God, their desire to give more and to give often grows. Why should we expect anything less? The divine principle of sowing and reaping means that you and I are called into a constantly expanding partnership with God to do His work by His power in the world.[1]

My friends Jerry and Pammie are an inspiring example of people who are choosing in faith to give more and to give often, knowing that God will replenish them to give still more. It seems every time we talk, they have another fascinating God Pocket story to share. Recently they told me about a nudge that came at a McDonald's drive-through window.

"We go there a lot in the mornings," says Jerry. "The other morning a girl named Brooke was at the window. We'd seen her there before. She was pregnant, just a few weeks from delivery. As we waited for her to hand us our order, I looked over at my wife and said, 'I think God wants us to do something with our God Pocket. What about you?' Pammie said, 'I agree. I'm thinking we should give fifty dollars.'"

Turns out, that's the exact amount Jerry had in mind. So as Brooke handed them their breakfast order, he said to her, "We feel like God wants us to give you this fifty dollars. It's not a tip. It's from God. Have a great day!" And he handed her the gift from their God Pocket. She was taken completely by surprise, of course, and overcome with gratitude.

A few days later, when Jerry and Pammie went through the McDonald's lane again, Brooke handed them a note that read, "I was truly touched by your gift the other day, and I'm so very thankful. I have been saving money for a car seat for my baby. But I was still fifty dollars short. Your gift gave me just what I need! ☺ Thank you again! Brooke."

If you met Jerry and Pammie, you would never guess that they started out feeling disqualified. "We were like a lot of people out there who feel as though they've failed God," says Jerry. "We felt like broken vessels. But Scripture shows us that God can be even more glorified in someone who has been broken. It's not what people think of us; it's what God thinks of us. It's not about the show; it's about God showing up!"

These days they describe themselves as "God's little people" who are being used to deliver financial miracles, not just here and there, but on a regular basis. Since they began partnering with God to deliver God Pockets, they have…

- delivered a God Pocket to a young man who told them he had been far from God. The next Sunday he came to their church, bringing three other visitors with him, and rededicated his life to Christ. "He told us his grandmother had been praying for him and she'd be so happy!"

- delivered a God Pocket that helped rescue, at the last minute, a destitute young woman from going to work in a strip club.

- seen family members get the God Pocket vision themselves. A brother and sister-in-law have involved their grandchildren in giving Pockets away. After seventy-seven-year-old Aunt Pauline came for a visit, she began delivering God Pockets too. Now she's teaching her friends to do the same.

- witnessed a God Pocket miracle that opened up a young man's heart to his need for Christ right in the middle of a restaurant. "He was so ready. He prayed the sinner's prayer right there at the table!" The young man has now gotten involved in a local church.

- seen a substantial God Pocket provide a new beginning for an acquaintance who was at the end of her rope. Tina had lost her job, but the God Pocket from Jerry and Pammie gave her hope. Then, through a remarkable chain of circumstances, God multiplied the original gift in her life so that now Tina is established in her own pet-grooming business. Tina now delivers God Pocket miracles to customers, and God has so prospered her business that she can barely keep up with the new clientele.

"Giving has become a delightful way of life for us," Jerry and Pammie wrote to me recently. "We see someone in need; God nudges; we quickly respond. Over the years we've observed that the more we increase our giving, the more God abundantly releases His financial blessings on us so we can give even more. God has truly withheld no good thing from us! We have literally been blessed in every area of our lives! We are a walking testimony of God's promised blessings to those who generously give to others in need."

What could *giving more* look like in your life?

Giving together

Churches are beginning to see in the God Pocket an accessible and motivating tool to encourage giving and outreach in their own communities. At a pastors' breakfast recently, I held up a leather God Pocket and showed it around. Then I turned it over so everyone could see the words "The God Pocket" embossed on the Pocket, and I explained how a specially designed pouch makes a terrific conversation starter and a natural giveaway. "How many of you think your people would catch a vision to do this as a church?"

Churches are beginning to see in the God Pocket an accessible and motivating tool to encourage giving and outreach.

Every hand went up. One pastor said he'd start with his youth group. "I love the way the God Pocket subtly teaches so many big ideas," he said. "The importance of giving to people in need, of course. But also listening for the Spirit's leading and doing real ministry as a lifestyle."

At their annual Christmas banquet, a church in Lexington, Kentucky, witnessed the launch of what they've called "the coolest God Pocket movement ever." Every one of the 230 people in attendance received a leather God Pocket, with funds already included, and instructions from the pastor on how to use it. "The pastor encouraged each of us to be sensitive to the God Nudges and ready to give in order to make a real impact for Him on our area," one participant recalled. Individuals and families came back with inspiring stories of what it was like to partner with God in personal giving. God Pocket appointments happened at a gas station, in restaurants, at an unemployed person's front door, at a fitness club.

"Since the God Pocket distribution at Christmas, people are taking note of the importance of being sensitive to the God Nudge," reports a church member. "And many here are becoming regular God Pocket Partners." I've heard similar stories from churches from the Carolinas to California.

Were you surprised that a God Pocket can be large enough to comfortably accommodate an SUV? A large church in downtown Orlando recently took the God Pocket even further. Brokenhearted by the high rate of foreclosures and resulting "new homelessness" within ten miles of their church, the members wanted to see what could happen when *a whole church becomes the God Pocket.* Here's what I mean: Even though their budget had been hit hard by a downturn in giving, the church asked God to meet the needs of those around them first *and through their own money devoted in advance to Him.* The result? In an unprecedented outpouring of love on just one week- end, the congregation gave and pledged a total of $5.6 million for the needy in their community!

"We believe we were put here by divine choice, and we have to make a difference," said the senior pastor.

Another pastor at the church said, "Seeing a miracle happen is an amazing thing. As the donations and pledges were coming in, I felt as if I had a grandstand seat to see God at work in the hearts and minds of His people."

IT BEGINS WITH ONE...

What could happen in our homes, churches, businesses, and community groups if we came together to show God's goodness to the world? What could happen among your circle of friends if you started a God Pocket small group, meeting regularly to encourage each other, to pray together, and even to make your own Pockets?

What would giving together on that scale look like? I'll tell you. It would look like the church of Jesus Christ is finally claiming its true calling in our world.

Imagine the impact on our nation if fifty thousand Partners asked God to lead them to at least one God Pocket delivery every month for a year. That would add up to six hundred thousand financial miracles! If a million Partners delivered a God Pocket every week for the next two years, the number would swell to more than a hundred million miracle encounters!

And what would *giving together* on that scale look like?

I'll tell you. It would look like the church of Jesus Christ is finally claiming another part of its true calling in our world—demonstrating compassion to those in need. It would look a lot more like the ministry of Jesus on earth. Do you remember how He described His mission?

The Spirit of the LORD is upon Me,
Because He has anointed Me
To preach the gospel to the poor;
He has sent Me to heal the brokenhearted,
To proclaim liberty to the captives
And recovery of sight to the blind,
To set at liberty those who are oppressed;
To proclaim the acceptable year of the LORD.[2]

Together, and with God's help, we can create an international movement of Christ's followers who are prepared every day to show His true heart to the world. What a stunning and altogether wonderful sight that would be!

Will you join me in reaching for very big things for God?

Start by asking yourself how many God Pockets you'd like to deliver for Him before the year is over. Then write it down, and ask Him to make it a reality in your life.

HOW TO BE A
GOD POCKET PARTNER

Join me in inviting others to be God Pocket Partners.

Here's how to give the invitation:

1 Open with intrigue. "Have you ever had a strong sense that God wanted you to say or give something to someone you met, but you weren't prepared...so you didn't do anything? Most people have."

2 Tell the big idea. "The God Pocket prepares you in advance to partner with God for a financial miracle. It's a special pocket or place in your wallet or purse where you carry money that you've devoted to God. That way you're ready when He leads you to deliver His gift to the person He has in mind."

3 Describe the preparation and presentation. "You prepare for a God Pocket encounter by taking seven easy-to-remember steps:

- You **decide** how much money you are going to place into your God Pocket.
- You **devote** that amount of money directly to God.
- You **deposit** your devoted money into your God Pocket.

- You **depend** on God to lead you to the exact person He has in mind. He does this by an inner push we call a "God Nudge."
- You **deliver** God's funds to the recipient.
- You **declare** that God is the ultimate Giver who provided the funds.
- You **disciple** the person who receives the God Pocket to become a delivery agent themselves.

4 **Show your Pocket.** "I use these specially produced God Pockets because they help the conversation happen more naturally." Or describe how you keep your devoted money in a special place in your wallet or purse.

5 **Share your experience.** "Let me share with you what happened once when I delivered a God Pocket..."

6 **Give a Pocket.** "If you sincerely desire to be a God Pocket Partner, I'd love to get you started by giving you my God Pocket!"

7 **Recommend this book.** "I'll send you the book that will tell you more. It's called *The God Pocket,* and it's short enough that you can read the whole thing in one sitting!"

Determine to give *differently,* give *more,* and give *together* as He leads.

Share the good news of the God Pocket with others.

And take a step right now to launch your new life as a God Pocket Partner. If you'll turn the page, I'll show you what that step is.

THE GOD POCKET
He owns it. You carry it. Suddenly, everything changes!

7

Your Next Step

Now is the moment. Heaven waits.
Will you make your move?

You stand on the brink of a very different life. Consider what you now know to be true:

You know that your God Pocket is an invitation for God to use you to reveal in an unforgettable way His goodness and generosity to people in need.

You know that the funds you carry in your God Pocket already belong to God; you are simply His humble delivery agent.

You know that you can be confident that God can and will connect you with the exact person He has in mind. All you have to do is stay dependent and alert.

You know that, as you give, God will resupply your resources. You will "have an abundance for every good work."[1]

Your God Pocket—you now realize—is like a mysterious doorway into an almost limitless life of joy in His service.

Are you ready?

If so, I invite you to take one simple, powerful step. I've recommended this action to thousands of Christians, with absolutely inspiring results:

Ask God to send you on a God Pocket Mission.

"HERE I AM. SEND ME!"

You might be wondering, *But I'm already committed to being a God Pocket Partner. Why should I ask to be sent?*

If you know your Bible, you know that you and I have already been "sent." Jesus described our mission to His disciples: "As the Father has sent Me, I also send you."

Later He restated the mission, this time as a command: "Go into all the world and preach the gospel to every creature."[2]

But there's a problem. Have you noticed? Millions of Christ's followers already *know* what Jesus said. Millions agree that, since Jesus commanded us to go, we *should* go. And millions are willing, prepared, and available to go.

Yet so few go.

I've asked audiences all over the world this simple question: "What percentage of God's people would you say actually respond when He puts them face to face with a divine appointment?" My audiences' responses are pretty consistent. Of one thousand people God might nudge to partner with Him

> Your God Pocket— you now realize—is like a mysterious doorway into an almost limitless life of joy in His service.

in a divinely arranged appointment, audiences say fewer than ten are likely to say yes.

What's the solution? What single action could you take so that you're not only *expecting* God to step into your day at any moment but you've *already decided to act* when He does?

In my experience, it's this: stand up in God's presence, raise your hand, and ask to be sent.

That's what Isaiah did. You might remember the well-known Bible passage where Isaiah describes what must have been the high point of his life—a real-time vision of what was happening in Heaven. In his riveting account, he describes what he saw:

> *I saw the Lord sitting on a throne, high and lifted up, and the train of His robe filled the temple.*[3]

The doorposts shake. The throne room is filled with smoke, filled with the cries of angels—and filled most of all with the wondrous presence of God. What an incredible sight!

Then, out of the noise and smoke, Isaiah hears God asking a question:

> *Whom shall I send,*
> *And who will go for Us?*

Isaiah may be just a spectator, but he doesn't hesitate to interrupt! He calls out, "Here am I! Send me."[24]

The Hebrew of Isaiah's response is an imperative. He wants so much to be sent that he almost *commands* God to send him. Of course, he can't possibly know where God might send him, and he doesn't ask. He just pleads to be the one God chooses.

God's response, too, is immediate. He commissions Isaiah to go to Israel and to call the people back to God. That one plea in God's presence changes everything for Isaiah, influences the course of a nation, and still inspires us today.

Isaiah's glimpse of Heaven reveals something about how God

> Stand up in God's presence, raise your hand, and ask to be sent.

works that I don't want you to miss: *God is urgently looking for people who want to do Heaven's work.* That picture—of a God who is seeking everywhere and at all times for eager volunteers—confirms one of the great themes of the Bible. From the first page to the last page, we see a God who searches for volunteers to stand in the gap for Him; go on missions of mercy; meet the needs of the weak, the broken, the hungry, and the destitute; and spread the gospel of Jesus Christ.[5] In fact, the Bible tells us that God looks "to and fro throughout the whole earth" for those who will say yes to Him.[6] It's not too extreme to say that God is *constantly seeking* people who will partner with Him to do Heaven's work on earth!

Do you want to be one of God's loyal servants? Your God Pocket might be small, but God will show Himself strong for you. He will multiply your few dollar bills as Jesus did the five loaves and two fish. With your yes, God can and will do wonders. You will not only witness these wonders; you will deliver them!

You have come to this page for a reason, my friend. Now is the moment. Heaven waits. God invites. Will you take your step?

YOUR NEW LIFE DELIVERING GOD POCKETS

Join me in these simple steps of asking God to choose and direct you in the days ahead as His own God Pocket delivery agent.

Consciously enter the throne room of Heaven. In your mind's eye, walk into the magnificent throne room where God the Father sits with Jesus Christ at His right hand. You are showing God that this is an important event in your life, not just words you pray.

Volunteer with the words "Here I am. Send me!" Picture yourself asking God with all your heart to choose you. That's all you need to say. For you, it is the "fervent prayer of a righteous man," and God will honor it.[7]

> **W**ith your yes, God can and will do wonders. You will not only witness these wonders; you will deliver them!

Precommit to act when you are nudged. Pledge to God what you will do with your God Pocket: "I am carrying Your provision. I am Your agent and ambassador. As You lead, I *will* respond." In the same way that devoting your money is a decision made in advance, precommitting to act when God nudges means you've already decided not to be distracted by excuses or doubt.

Actively put your faith in God to lead you to a God Pocket miracle soon. Exercise your faith by affirming to God, "I

trust You. I can depend on You to show Yourself strong...
through me!" And He will.

Now you are done. Leave the throne room with joy.
You are a sent one in God's service.

I have asked God to send me on a regular basis for
years, and I encourage you to do the same. Write out a
commitment like the one that follows to express your new
status as a sent servant, God Pocket in hand. Post your
pledge on your mirror, tape it on your dashboard or desk,
or write it across your daily planner.

Then make it a regular—even daily—prayer until it
comes to describe your new life delivering God Pocket
miracles for Him.

MY GOD POCKET PRAYER

Dear God,

Today I ask to be sent to show Your love and
deliver Your funds to the person You choose.
I carry Your provision in my God Pocket, and
I am ready and willing. I am Your servant, Lord.

Whenever You nudge me, I will respond! Here
am I—please send me!

My friend, I know He will, because, as we've written
at the bottom of every chapter…

THE GOD POCKET
He owns it. You carry it. Suddenly, everything changes!

ACKNOWLEDGMENTS

This little book represents an enormous commitment on the part of so many. I'm especially grateful for the ministry partnership of Jill Milligan, executive director of the Exponential Group; Jerry and Pammie Turner (my first God Pocket Partners); and Bruce and Toni Hebel of Forgiving Forward. Your sincere enthusiasm for the message of *The God Pocket* has borne a lot of fruit. Many thanks! The publishing, production, sales, and marketing teams at WaterBrook Multnomah have brought energy and a commitment to excellence to this project— along with plenty of patience. Thank you all! I have been blessed again to work with my collaborator, David Kopp, and we have both benefited again from the excellent contributions from his wife, Heather. Our friendship is a gift. My daughter, Jessica Cozzens, played a key role during the development of this book and the workbook for the God Pocket course that goes with it. Thank you so much for the creativity and joy you always bring.

And most of all to Darlene, my gracious wife and life partner—thank you for your insights, support, love, and, as always, your steadfast prayers. We couldn't have done it without you!

Notes

Chapter 1: Heaven Leans Down
1. See Ephesians 3:20–21, NJKV.

Chapter 2: How the God Pocket Works
1. Psalm 50:10
2. Romans 10:13–15
3. 1 Timothy 6:18

Chapter 3: Was That a Nudge?
1. Consider these examples: Moses (Exodus 3:1–4:17), Gideon (Judges 6), Jeremiah (Jeremiah 1), Paul (Acts 9:1–9)—even Jesus (Matthew 26:36–46)!

Chapter 4: Agents in Action
1. See Isaiah 53.
2. See Psalm 16:11.

Chapter 5: The Mystery of Multiplying
1. Proverbs 19:17
2. The bracketed words are the author's commentary.
3. See Proverbs 15:33; 14:23; 16:6.
4. Proverbs 11:25; 22:9, NIV
5. 2 Corinthians 9:6–8

6. 2 Corinthians 9:8, author's paraphrase

7. My book *A Life God Rewards* explores God's amazing promises of repayment in eternity.

8. For example, see Matthew 16:27; 19:21; Luke 6:22–24; 14:14.

9. Luke 14:13–14

10. 1 Timothy 6:18–19

11. See Philippians 4:19.

12. See Matthew 6:19–20.

Chapter 6: The Generosity Conspiracy

1. See 2 Corinthians 9:6–13.

2. Luke 4:18–19

Chapter 7: Your Next Step

1. 2 Corinthians 9:8

2. John 20:21; Mark 16:15

3. Isaiah 6:1

4. Isaiah 6:8

5. Responding to God's calls are Ezekiel (Ezekiel 22:30), Isaiah (Isaiah 6), Jonah (Jonah 1:1; 3:1), Philip (Acts 8:26), Peter (Acts 10:19–20); those helping the needy (Matthew 25:31–46); and those spreading the gospel (Matthew 28:18–20).

6. 2 Chronicles 16:9

7. James 5:16

WELCOME TO GOD POCKET PARTNERS!

Join with others who are discovering the joys of partnering with God to show His goodness to the world. At www.TheGodPocket.com, you'll discover a community of like-minded Partners, along with resources you'll need to spread our conspiracy of God-directed generosity to families, churches, and communities around the world.

- **Share your God Pocket story.** Take a moment to read the stories of other God Pocket delivery agents and write your latest God Pocket story. That way, God can use you to inspire thousands of others to partner with Him today. And you'll be blessed all over again in the telling! Go to www.TheGodPocket.com and click on "My God Pocket Story."

- **Select your own God Pocket.** Many delivery agents have found that using a separate God Pocket makes giving God's money feel more natural and opens the way for relaxed, ministry-oriented conversations. At www.TheGodPocket.com, you'll find a range of appealing, inexpensive God Pockets to use and pass along, from colorful cardstock to embossed leather. All are available in single-item or bulk orders.

- **Start a conversation.** To download free discussion starters for personal study or small-group use, go to www.TheGodPocket.com.

- **Order the God Pocket DVD course for your church or small group.** Join Bruce Wilkinson as he teaches the exciting six-part God Pocket video series— taking you and your friends far beyond the book. Watch memorable skits and experience practical, hands-on God Pocket training with the course workbook. Order by calling 704-522-7221 or going to www.TheGodPocket.com.

- **Schedule a God Pocket Seminar.** Certified instructors are ready to conduct either a Saturday or Sunday God Pocket Seminar for your church, retreat, or organization. Call 704-522-7221 to find out more. www.TheGodPocket.com

ABOUT THE AUTHORS

One of the world's foremost Christian teachers, **Bruce Wilkinson** is best known as the author of the *New York Times* #1 bestseller *The Prayer of Jabez.* He is also the author of other bestsellers, including *You Were Born for This, A Life God Rewards, Secrets of the Vine,* and *The Dream Giver.* Over the past three decades, Wilkinson has founded numerous global ministry and humanitarian initiatives, including, most recently, orphan care and AIDS education in Africa. Bruce and his wife, Darlene Marie, have three children and several grandchildren. They live outside Atlanta.

David Kopp has collaborated with Bruce Wilkinson on more than a dozen best-selling books, including *The Prayer of Jabez.* He is an editor and writer living in Colorado.

He Owns It. You Carry It.

Get the Simple Tool that Can Help You Deliver a Blessing!

GodPocket

This small convenient pocket allows you to manage the gifts God has entrusted to you–and provides a discreet way to deliver a blessing.

- Available in various colors
- Choose from: leather, vinyl or burlap
- Fits easily in your pocket or purse

LAWYERS

WAYNE F. HILL

AND

CYNTHIA J. ÖTTCHEN

—

ILLUSTRATIONS

BY

TOM LULEVITCH

EBURY PRESS · LONDON

3 5 7 9 10 8 6 4 2

First published in the United Kingdom in 1996 by
Ebury Press
Random House
20 Vauxhall Bridge Road
London SW1V 2SA.

Random House Australia (Pty) Limited
20 Alfred Street, Milsons Point, Sydney,
New South Wales 2061, Australia

Random House New Zealand Limited
18 Poland Road, Glenfield,
Auckland 10, New Zealand

Random House South Africa (Pty) Limited
Endulini, 5A Jubilee Road, Parktown 2193, South Africa

Random House UK Limited Reg. No. 954009

A CIP catalogue record for this book is available from
the British Library

ISBN: 0 09 180960 6

Designed by Alexander Knowlton
@ BEST Design Incorporated
Illustrations by Tom Lulevitch

Printed and bound in Great Britain by
Mackays of Chatham PLC, Chatham, Kent

This book is dedicated
to two lawyers of our
acquaintance who have
succeeded against all odds
at becoming normal
human beings. Their success
has only made the goal
seem attainable for others,
thus tormenting the legal
profession. This is a double
achievement, and it moves us
to pay double respect: first in
mentioning them and second
in honoring their request
for anonymity. We only regret
that the supreme desire
of lawyers to be like everyone
else has lured one of these
attorneys toward politics.

The first thing we do,

let's kill all the lawyers.

HENRY VI, PART 2

CONTENTS

Introduction   9
On Lawyers   15
  Counsel and Advice   17
  Trial Performance   22
  Legal Fees   27
On Clients   31
  Threatening Legal Action   33
  Verdicts and Sentences   37
  The Client from Hell   42
Distinctive Qualities
  Attributed to All Lawyers   47
  Verbose   50
  Litigious   54
  Tricky   58
  Dishonest   62
  Insincere   64
  Pompous   67
  Obstructionist   70
  Incompetent   72
  Image Conscious   76
Conclusion   79

INTRODUCTION

All the oldest trades share

one distinctive quality.

They pride themselves in

doing anything for a fee.

We know therefore that law is an

extremely ancient profession.

Emerging from the dim origins

of human experience, a lawyer

will complain on demand—

before, during, or after the fact.

Any fact at all. Or sometimes before, during, and after no facts whatever. A lawyer is a vacuum. You can hire one, insert your problem into the void, and, bingo, become the proud possessor of a case.

Unfortunately, a habit of suspicion, hostility, ingratitude, prejudice, ignorance, prudishness, arrogance, greed, lust, anger, gluttony, envy, and perhaps not a little sloth keeps normal people from recognizing what any trained legal mind understands intuitively—that the oldest professions deserve the greatest honor (and appropriate remuneration). This impasse of communication has caused a prolonged and tragic state of cold war. Therefore we have drafted a peace plan. In this slim volume we hope to achieve what has so long proven elusive: a mutual understanding between lawyers and the human race.

There is common ground, and it lies in the texts of the one figure whose genius is great enough to accommodate all interests: William Shakespeare. Remember that "all the world's a stage and all the men and women merely players." Shakespeare brought to the stage every conceivable human type, and he deals with every possible kind of human conflict—just as lawyers do. In the Bard's expressions of opposition, we find our mutual language.

In Shakespeare's 38 plays there are approximately ten thousand insults, and those we have selected for this book create an environment for constructive participation by both parties. If you are not a lawyer, Shakespeare will open your eyes and ears to the contentious world of attorneys and lend you all the necessary wit to speak your mind in the wide human territory covered by the legal trade. Memorize a few of Shakespeare's slurs, and you'll never be at a loss for words, even among the professionals. If you are a lawyer, these insults offer a razor's edge on your performance at the bar.

Insults are at the heart of the legal system because the purpose of law in democracy is to spread blame. Law champions the high rhetoric of justice and humane punishment, but it is actually a clever scheme for washing one's hands of responsibility, hiding in a crowd, and dodging responsibility. Once you've secured a whole system of strangers to trounce your enemy, it is harder for him or her to retaliate against you personally. The lawyer's job is to round up as big a mob of "experts" and well-coached witnesses as possible (stretching back in time, this cloud of witnesses is called "precedent"), and the party with the biggest party wins.

Making this spectacle possible is a vast profession of faceless middlemen and -women paid to be neutral and civil to the guilty while collecting evidence for lawyers to tear apart. Invariably respectful, law officers are the only ones excluded from the pleasure of hurling insults, although Shakespeare's wit can allow even them to try out a few less obvious remarks. They need not feel deprived, for they are doubly compensated for their neutrality: mercifully spared from unemployment and from ethical reflection. This second is achieved by official use of the phrase "I'm just doing my job," which is as much as most people care about what is just. For those who do care, justice is a synonym for smugness if you're a winner and for green-eyed envy if you're not.

The goal is not to agree but to win. It's in court, at a trial, that the hand-washing shows up at its cleanest. Everyone present has someone else to take the blame. The naturally aggressive plaintiffs or defendants sit silent while their lawyers cut and thrust, the lawyers go quiet before the judge, and the judge waits patiently for the jury (which represents everybody)—so ultimately the blame pours out into the great common sump of humanity. This corroborates the other fact of legal life: since human society is the source of all human behavior, what anybody does is ultimately everybody's fault. Everyone is guilty; everyone is innocent; and lawyers send out the bills.

Because law is bent on spreading blame, our discovery of a trove of wit, by the acknowledged genius of the bristly remark, is a breakthrough in the long struggle between lawyers and normal people. All can now drink at the same waterhole, not to say the same bar. As the title declares, this array of Shakespeare's insults for lawyers is effective in both senses—for them to give and for them to get. The historic importance of this mutual manual far exceeds—and is only increased by—its eminently portable size.

ON LAWYERS

How now, my sweet

creature of bombast?

HENRY IV, PART 1
2. 4. 322–23

STRIVING TOO HARD TO BE HUMAN, lawyers have a distorted idea of what it is to be people. They have singled out only one defining human activity to emulate: complaining. Most of us enjoy indulging in a bit of gossip and bitchery from time to time, but that isn't all we do. Lawyers, however, have excessively literal minds. They have made a full-time occupation of turning acrimony, spite, and blame-passing into a public art.

There is a reason why the advice a lawyer gives strikes us the way it does. Law is made by political consensus (like sausage-making, it is not a process anyone with a principled stomach wants to watch). Lawmakers are models of the species who represent everyone else. Legislatures are upside-down juries —chosen to talk rather than listen. Not only does law therefore originate from all of us, but law is applied by precedent. Over the years the law takes on the wrinkles, scars, and puffy flacidity of day-after-day to-ing and fro-ing, in-ing and out-ing—just as people do.

The upshot is that in both its creation and

its practice, the law is the essence of ourselves. A distinguished lawyer professionally advises us on ourselves, then, drawing on our own experience. Because the lawyer's very presence means we have not roused the courage enough to counsel *ourselves* ourselves, this person who steps in to represent us in giving us our own advice has little chance of making sense. Or, more surreal yet, the lawyer may make perfect sense. In either case, apart from some chancy tricks for outfoxing other lawyers, the advice we get glimmers in a mist of déjà vu somewhere between light musical entertainment and modern art. A few lines from Shakespeare can settle our nerves.

One may smile, and smile, and be a villain.

HAMLET
1. 5. 108

[You] only are reputed wise
for saying nothing.

THE MERCHANT OF VENICE
1. 1. 96–97

What thou professest, a baboon,
could he speak,
Would own a name too dear.

PERICLES
4. 6. 177–78

Where we are, there's daggers in men's smiles.

MACBETH
2. 3. 139–40

I pray thee cease thy counsel,
Which falls into mine ears as profitless
As water in a sieve.

MUCH ADO ABOUT NOTHING
5. 1. 3–5

He that depends
Upon your favours, swims with fins of lead,
And hews down oaks with rushes.

CORIOLANUS
1. 1. 178–80

I find the ass in compound with the major
part of your syllables.

CORIOLANUS
2. 1. 57–58

Thou half-penny purse of wit,
thou pigeon-egg of discretion.

LOVE'S LABOUR'S LOST
5. 1. 69–70

You put sharp weapons
in a madman's hands.

HENRY VI, PART 2
3. 1. 347

In the managing of quarrels you may
say he is wise; for either he avoids them
with great discretion, or undertakes
them with a most Christian-like fear.

MUCH ADO ABOUT NOTHING
2. 3. 183–86

Thy lips rot off!

TIMON OF ATHENS
4. 3. 64

I profit not by thy talk.

TROILUS AND CRESSIDA
5. 1. 13

[I] allowed your approach rather to
wonder at you than to hear you.

TWELFTH NIGHT
1. 5. 199–200

TRIAL PERFORMANCE

IT IS NEVER THE DEFENDANT who is on trial but the lawyer who is in performance. A satirist or cynic might whiff injustice in this fact and point an accusing finger at the deep affection of the masses for bread and circuses, but the truth remains that the best box seats are in the jury box. It was inevitable that courtrooms would eventually sport video cameras. There's big money in broadcasting the spectacle to the rest of humanity, who are unfettered by the silence imposed upon jurors. Those of us in the social gene pool for the jury box, who happen to be passing an operating television set, can shout abuse and mutter innuendo at the performers. We the TV audience judge all things in the end. With the Bard ringing majestically in our minds, we also judge the lawyers. Herein is justice enough to satisfy any cynic.

The unflattering evidence from the video cameras proves that playwrights do courtroom scenes better than stand-up lawyers improvising possibly could. Playwrights—with the benefit of scripts, rehearsals, rewrites, and editing—naturally depict human life better than anyone who has only one chance to struggle through it live. So-called courtroom drama is actually just plain drama. One person will come away from a trial filled with appreciation, while another equally intelligent, cultured, and worldly wise individual will emerge outraged. There is no satisfactory scientific explanation for this phenomenon, and so the achievement will continue to be ascribed to pure legal genius. Our suspicion, however, is that it has everything to do with show business.

> *[You] quarrel in print, by the book; as you have books for good manners.*
>
> **AS YOU LIKE IT**
> **5. 4. 89–90**

> *Your helps are many, or else your actions would grow wondrous single: your abilities are too infant-like for doing much alone.*
>
> **CORIOLANUS**
> **2. 1. 34–37**

You wear out a good wholesome forenoon in hearing a cause between an orange-wife and a faucet-seller, and then rejourn the controversy of threepence to a second day of audience. When you are hearing a matter between party and party, if you chance to be pinched with the colic, you make faces like mummers, against all patience, and, in roaring for a chamber-pot, dismiss the controversy bleeding, the more entangled by your hearing. All the peace you make in their cause is calling both the parties knaves.

CORIOLANUS
2. 1. 69–79

I muse you make so slight a question.

HENRY IV, PART 2
4. 1. 167

O, I smell false Latin.

LOVE'S LABOUR'S LOST
5. 1. 75

A knavish speech sleeps in a foolish ear.

HAMLET
4. 2. 22–23

His complexion is perfect gallows.

THE TEMPEST

1. 1. 29

Away, I do condemn mine ears
that have so long attended thee.

CYMBELINE
1. 7. 141–42

His purse is empty already,
all's golden words are spent.

HAMLET
5. 2. 129–30

Your bait of falsehood takes this carp of truth.

HAMLET
2. 1. 63

It offends me to the soul to hear a robustious
periwig-pated fellow tear a passion to tatters.

HAMLET
3. 2. 8–10

Are these the breed of wits so wonder'd at?

LOVE'S LABOUR'S LOST
5. 2. 266

[You] prattle something too wildly.

THE TEMPEST
3. 1. 57–58

Wilt thou show the whole wealth
of thy wit in an instant?

THE MERCHANT OF VENICE

3. 5. 50–51

This petty brabble will undo us all.

TITUS ANDRONICUS

2. 1. 62

There's a stewed phrase indeed!

TROILUS AND CRESSIDA

3. 1. 40–41

No more of these vain parleys.

THE TWO NOBLE KINSMEN

3. 3. 10

They are now in a most extravagant vagary.

THE TWO NOBLE KINSMEN

4. 3. 67–68

LEGAL FEES

JUST AS EVERYONE LIKES to complain, everyone also has an opinion about what's fair and what isn't. That makes justice different in every case. And therein lies the profit.

There is always room for litigation because justice is whatever you want, and injustice is someone else having it. Naturally lawyers, striving to be like everyone else, want to have opinions too. They go to school to learn how to look things up and how to sell a second-hand argument previously used by a long line of old codgers, also known as "precedent." If they win a case, they drink to justice. If they lose, they magnanimously offer to take more of our money for a shot at overturning such an obvious injustice as someone else now having what we want.

Shakespeare is the ideal peace broker. He provides congenial company for lawyers, for hardly anything is known of him personally, and what "Shakespeare says" is only what he makes his myriad characters say. In one particular, however, lawyers come into the open and prosecute their own interests. Their furtive and slippery life is thrown into dramatic relief in the following instance:

Lawyers who *lose* have the temerity to send out bills anyway.

Anyone else would slink away and find something to stanch the flow of embarrassment. But under the inspired guise of discretion itself, a characteristic lawyers do not possess, they send bills in the same dignified envelopes that serve up threats and other notices of unsavory portent. Such ominous envelopes delivered alongside nonthreatening mail arouse questions (and a foretaste of public exposure) in curious or suspicious minds. But lawyers themselves are immune to embarrassment, for all such correspondence arriving at their premises must be dismissed as relating to clients or as invitations to lunch with colleagues. Lawyers invoice with impunity because they dine at the top of the rumor chain.

The one fixed purpose driving all lawyers is power and money—which amount to the same thing. While lawyers uphold this shining beacon of their trade, there is always a multiplicity of new issues to fight about. There is never a lack of business, and there is always room for more lawyers. In fact, we are the authors of the modest proposal that everyone should be made a lawyer. This idea, incidentally, has even gained the support of the opposition: the unenlightened curmudgeons who would love to see the law trade wiped out in a single stroke.

Let's meet as little as we can.

AS YOU LIKE IT
3. 2. 253

The benefit which thou shalt reap
is such a name whose repetition
will be dogg'd with curses.

CORIOLANUS
5. 3. 142–44

Take you me for a sponge?

HAMLET
4. 2. 13

If I owe you any thing
I will pay you in cudgels.

HENRY V
5. 1. 67

A knot you are of damned bloodsuckers.

RICHARD III
3. 3. 6

ON CLIENTS

Grovel on thy face.

HENRY VI, PART 2
1. 2. 9

A LAWYER'S VIEW OF THE WORLD is distorted—by people. Even a little experience with humankind sours the normal self-satisfied optimism that causes us to describe the most widespread and general of human behavior as "inhuman." We seize upon the decent and the generous, celebrate acts of kindness and nominate them for awards.

But these are rarities among humans that lawyers almost never see. For better or worse, one's profession molds one's outlook on the world. Walking down the same street anywhere, doctors see maladies. Tyrants see rivals. Salesmen, suckers. Cops, crooks. Psychoanalysts, themselves. Botanists, no one at all. And invariably, lawyers see sordid guilt and patched-up excuses, prompting them to borrow retorts liberally from Shakespeare. They cannot avoid looking upon their own clients with the same world-weary eyes through which they see the opposition.

Your oaths
Are words, and poor conditions but unseal'd.

ALL'S WELL THAT ENDS WELL
4. 2. 29-30

I will no further offend you
than becomes me for my good.

AS YOU LIKE IT
1. 1. 79-80

Sell when you can,
you are not for all markets.

AS YOU LIKE IT
3. 5. 60

I should once name you derogately.

ANTONY AND CLEOPATRA
2. 2. 33-34

Their tongues rot that speak against us!

ANTONY AND CLEOPATRA
3. 7. 15-16

I shall unfold equal discourtesy
to your best kindness.

CYMBELINE
2. 3. 97-98

O, there has been much
throwing about of brains.

HAMLET
2. 2. 356

You tread upon my patience.

HENRY IV, PART 1

1. 3. 4

For living murmurers there's places of rebuke.

HENRY VIII

2. 2. 130–31

Behold, behold,
where Madam Mitigation comes!

MEASURE FOR MEASURE

1. 2. 41

If you spend word for word with me,
I shall make your wit bankrupt.

THE TWO GENTLEMEN OF VERONA

2. 4. 37–38

If thy offences were upon record,
Would it not shame thee, in so fair a troop,
To read a lecture of them?

RICHARD II

4. 1. 230–32

Will you not eat your word?

MUCH ADO ABOUT NOTHING

4. 1. 277

Thy best props are warped!

THE TWO NOBLE KINSMEN
3. 2. 32

We honour you with trouble.

THE WINTER'S TALE
5. 3. 9

VERDICTS AND SENTENCES

EVERYONE ACTS LIKE A JUDGE, but not everyone acts like a lawyer acting like a judge. We freely convict the luckless creatures who happen to attract charges and appear handcuffed, raincoats over their heads, being dragged across the evening news. We are always beneficent and circumspect in our convictions. Lawyers take a different approach. For them the guilt or innocence of their neighbors is linked inseparably to delusions of heroic careers. Lawyers live and breathe the law, and dream in judges' phrases. Losses haunt their night sweats, and wildly imagined courtroom victories resound in benchlike tones across the peaceful unconscious miles.

Some lawyers, upon waking in the middle of a trial, aspire to be actual judges. Such attorneys will benefit most of all from the practice Shakespeare offers here. It's the sage phrase effortlessly tossed off that builds a firm judicial reputation and earns respect.

You would answer very well to a whipping.

ALL'S WELL THAT ENDS WELL
2. 2. 50–51

Keep him dark and safely locked.

ALL'S WELL THAT ENDS WELL
4. 1. 102–3

He hath out-villain'd villainy so far
that the rarity redeems him.

ALL'S WELL THAT ENDS WELL
4. 3. 264–65

O, if men were to be saved by merit,
what hole in hell were hot enough for [you]?

HENRY IV, PART 1
1. 2. 104–5

[You are] a ruffian that will swear, drink, dance,
Revel the night, rob, murder, and commit
The oldest sins the newest kind of ways.

HENRY IV, PART 2
4. 5. 124–26

[Your] offence is rank, it smells to heaven.

HAMLET

3. 3. 36

In the world's wide mouth
Live scandaliz'd and foully spoken of.

HENRY IV, PART 1

1. 3. 151–52

Thou art only mark'd for the hot vengeance
and the rod of heaven.

HENRY IV, PART 1

3. 2. 9–10

His few bad words are matched
with as few good deeds.

HENRY V

3. 2. 40–41

[You are] no better than a fellow of no merits.

HENRY V

5. 1. 7–8

[You are] a sort of naughty persons,
lewdly bent.

HENRY VI, PART 2

2. 1. 159

[You are] now muddied in Fortune's mood,
and smell somewhat strong
of her strong displeasure.

ALL'S WELL THAT ENDS WELL
5. 2. 4–5

I will not excuse you, you shall not be
excused, excuses shall not be admitted,
there is no excuse shall serve,
you shall not be excused.

HENRY IV, PART 2
5. 1. 4–6

All that is within [you] does condemn
itself for being there.

MACBETH
5. 2. 24–25

Beg that thou may'st have leave
to hang thyself.

THE MERCHANT OF VENICE
4. 1. 360

For thy life let justice be accus'd.

THE MERCHANT OF VENICE
4. 1. 129

Nothing emboldens sin so much as mercy.

TIMON OF ATHENS

3. 5. 3

[Your] grossness little characters sum up!

TROILUS AND CRESSIDA

1. 3. 324–25

THE CLIENT FROM HELL

WHEN PEOPLE STOPPED IMAGINING hell as being immediately underfoot, hell was rather flippantly declared to be within oneself, but that's no longer to be believed.

Hell could not possibly be within ourselves because hell is always in the company of lawyers.

Hell is meant to be a rather annoying place where things don't quite work out and a lot of people bother each other. Such conflict, as we know, is expressed through insults, and when insults take their most official form it's always in the language of the legal trade.

The client from hell abuses this cosmic order by arrogantly seeking to seize the pitchfork from the attorney's more able hands.

Such a "common customer" assumes he knows more than the lawyer, or appoints himself judge, jury, and executioner by blaming the lawyer when things go unexpectedly—or, worst of all, is anything but enthusiastic and instant about payment.

Every old theologian knows that even the devil is not omniscient. The reason the fiend does not know all is that infernal clients refuse to tell all. These amateurs, beguiled by their own complaints, have come to believe that they know better than the certified attorney. This thoroughly unprofessional failure of confidence foils the lawyer's best efforts and justifies plying clients with Shakespearean insults.

> *[I am] subject to the breath*
> *Of every fool, whose sense no more can feel*
> *But his own wringing!*
>
> **HENRY V**
> 4. 1. 240–42

O wonderful, when devils tell the truth!

RICHARD III

1. 2. 73

He that will give
good words to thee will flatter
Beneath abhorring.

CORIOLANUS
1. 1. 166–67

Ha! Mak'st thou this shame thy pastime?

KING LEAR
2. 4. 5–6

All the fiends of hell divide
themselves between you!

CYMBELINE
2. 4. 129–30

No more, you petty spirits of region low,
offend our hearing.

CYMBELINE
5. 4. 93–94

I do not like your faults.

JULIUS CAESAR
4. 3. 88

All in vain comes counsel to his ear.

RICHARD II
2. 1. 4

He may keep his own grace,
but he's almost out of mine, I can assure him.

HENRY IV, PART 2
1. 2. 27–28

Well, the truth is you live in great infamy.

HENRY IV, PART 2
1. 2. 135–36

Hell is empty,
And all the devils are here.

THE TEMPEST
1. 2. 214–15

Words pay no debts.

TROILUS AND CRESSIDA
3. 2. 55

DISTINCTIVE QUALITIES ATTRIBUTED TO ALL LAWYERS

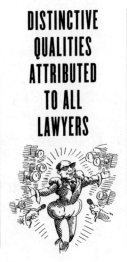

Come, come,

you talk greasily;

your lips grow foul.

LOVE'S LABOUR'S LOST
4. 1. 136

WHEN WE LUMP all lawyers into a stereotype, you would expect them to rise as one, indignant against so insensitive a disregard for their enduring contributions to the simulation of humanity. We might even get sued. But if some fine attorney rises up, a voice for the whole affronted profession, then we would rest our case. We win. No one could file a class action without admitting that attorneys actually *are* all exactly alike (the colorful ones are merely charging more). It takes a certain basic kind of person to learn just enough about real work not to do it—but to bluff and threaten with apparent authority and sway a jury of nonexperts. In other words, lawyers are actors.

It is well known that acting is a real job. Lawyers come close to being real people after all, just like everybody else. Each case is a play (or more likely these days a television soap opera), and everyone has a role. Real life, like the theater and the courtroom, is a contrived network of conflicts. The true art of living is the well-crafted insult.

If you do not know a lawyer to insult, select any person who speaks floridly, charges heinously, takes offense instantly, proceeds tactically, obfuscates smilingly, advises cautiously, promises hedgingly, swears forkedly, loiters majestically, moves sluggishly, bumbles with dignity, and dresses for the press. Certainly you'll be able to choose from at least a dozen people of that description, which proves that, like everyone else, you are surrounded by lawyers.

VERBOSE

If their purgation did consist in words,
They are as innocent as grace itself.

AS YOU LIKE IT
1. 3. 49–50

Brevity is the soul of wit,
And tediousness the limbs
and outward flourishes.

HAMLET
2. 2. 90–91

He draweth out the thread of his verbosity
finer than the staple of his argument.

LOVE'S LABOUR'S LOST
5. 1. 17–18

Thy lips shall sweep the ground.

HENRY VI, PART 2

4. 1. 74

Talk thy tongue weary.

CYMBELINE
3. 4. 113

More matter with less art.

HAMLET
2. 2. 94

How quaint an orator you are.

HENRY VI, PART 2
3. 2. 273

*They have been at a great feast of languages,
and stolen the scraps.*

LOVE'S LABOUR'S LOST
5. 1. 37–38

*What cracker is this same that
deafs our ears
With this abundance of superfluous breath?*

KING JOHN
2. 1. 147–48

*His words are a very fantastical banquet,
just so many strange dishes.*

MUCH ADO ABOUT NOTHING
2. 3. 20–21

Zounds! I was never
so bethump'd with words
Since I first call'd my brother's father dad.

KING JOHN
2. 1. 466–67

[This] is a tale
Told by an idiot, full of sound and fury,
Signifying nothing.

MACBETH
5. 5. 26–28

He hath a killing tongue and a quiet sword;
by the means whereof he breaks words, and
keeps whole weapons.

HENRY V
3. 2. 35–37

He speaks plain cannon, fire,
and smoke, and bounce;
He gives the bastinado with his tongue.

KING JOHN
2. 1. 462–63

[You] speak an infinite deal of nothing.

THE MERCHANT OF VENICE
1. 1. 113

How every fool can play upon the word!

THE MERCHANT OF VENICE

3. 5. 40

*He is a gentleman that loves to hear himself
talk, and will speak more in a minute than
he will stand to in a month.*

ROMEO AND JULIET

2. 4. 144–46

LITIGIOUS

*[You] brace of unmeriting, proud,
violent, testy magistrates!*

CORIOLANUS

2. 1. 42–43

*[You are] a stony adversary,
an inhuman wretch,
Uncapable of pity, void, and empty
From any dram of mercy.*

THE MERCHANT OF VENICE

4. 1. 4–6

O polish'd perturbation!

HENRY IV, PART 2

4. 5. 22

No man's pie is freed from
[your] ambitious finger.

HENRY VIII
1. 1. 52–53

*There is no more mercy in him
than there is milk in a male tiger.*

CORIOLANUS
5. 4. 28–29

*Grace thou wilt have none, no, by my troth,
not so much as will serve to be prologue
to an egg and butter.*

HENRY IV, PART 1
1. 2. 17–21

*[I am] weary of [your] dainty
and such picking grievances.*

HENRY IV, PART 2
4. 1. 197–98

*Thy head is as full of quarrels as an egg is
full of meat, and yet thy head hath been
beaten as addle as an egg for quarrelling.*

ROMEO AND JULIET
3. 1. 22–24

[You] partakers of a little gain!

HENRY VI, PART 1
2. 1. 52

Thou hid'st a thousand daggers
in thy thoughts,
Which thou hast whetted
on thy stony heart,
To stab at half an hour of my life.

HENRY IV, PART 2
4. 5. 106–8

Ye were ever good at sudden condemnations.

HENRY VIII
5. 2. 156

Besides that he's a fool, he's a great
quarreller; and but that he hath
the gift of a coward to allay the gust
he hath in quarrelling, 'tis thought among
the prudent he would
quickly have the gift of a grave.

TWELFTH NIGHT
1. 3. 29–33

They are arrant knaves, and will backbite.

HENRY IV, PART 2
5. 1. 30

TRICKY

*Three great oaths would scarce
make that be believed.*

ALL'S WELL THAT ENDS WELL
4. 1. 58–59

*Whatsoever cunning fiend it was
That wrought upon thee so preposterously
Hath got the voice in hell for excellence.*

HENRY V
2. 2. 111–13

[Thou art] not at all a friend to truth.

HENRY VIII
2. 4. 81–82

*They shoot but calm words
folded up in smoke,
To make a faithless error of your ears.*

KING JOHN
2. 1. 229–30

Confusion now hath made his masterpiece!

MACBETH
2. 3. 67

I am well acquainted with your manner of
wrenching the true cause the false way.

HENRY IV, PART 2
2. 1. 107–9

I have within my mind
A thousand raw tricks of these bragging Jacks,
Which I will practise.

THE MERCHANT OF VENICE
3. 4. 76–78

He will lie, sir, with such volubility that you
would think truth were a fool.

ALL'S WELL THAT ENDS WELL
4. 3. 244–45

O dear discretion,
how his words are suited!
The fool hath planted in his memory
An army of good words, and I do know
Of many fools that stand in better place,
Garnish'd like him, that for a tricksy word
Defy the matter.

THE MERCHANT OF VENICE
3. 5. 59–64

Seems he a dove?
His feathers are but borrow'd.

HENRY VI, PART 2
3. 1. 75

These lies are like their father that begot them,
gross as a mountain, open, palpable.

HENRY IV, PART 1
2. 4. 220–21

[You are] two yoke-devils sworn
to either's purpose.

HENRY V
2. 2. 106

You do advance your cunning
more and more.

THE MERRY WIVES OF WINDSOR
3. 2. 128

His gift is in devising impossible slanders.

MUCH ADO ABOUT NOTHING
2. 1. 128

What impossible matter will he
make easy next?

THE TEMPEST
2. 1. 85

[You] corrupter of words!

TWELFTH NIGHT
3. 1. 37

You undergo too strict a paradox,
Striving to make an ugly deed look fair.

TIMON OF ATHENS
3. 5. 24–25

This has been some stair-work,
some trunk-work, some behind-door-work.

THE WINTER'S TALE
3. 3. 73–75

DISHONEST

He has everything that an honest man
should not have; what an honest man should
have, he has nothing.

ALL'S WELL THAT ENDS WELL
4. 3. 250–52

The tongues of men are full of deceits.

HENRY V
5. 2. 117–18

That's villainous, and shows a most pitiful
ambition in the fool that uses it.

HAMLET
3. 2. 43–45

The benefit that thou shalt reap
is such a name whose repetition will be
dogg'd with curses.

CORIOLANUS
5. 3. 142–44

How cheerfully on the false trail they cry.

HAMLET
4. 5. 109

Thy fall hath left a kind of blot,
To mark the full-fraught man
and best indued
With some suspicion.

HENRY V
2. 2. 138–40

You have as little honesty as honour.

HENRY VIII
3. 2. 271

As low as to thy heart through the false
passage of thy throat thou liest.

RICHARD II
1. 1. 124–25

God and good men hate so foul a liar.

RICHARD II

1. 1. 114

You lie, like dogs, and yet say nothing neither.

THE TEMPEST

3. 2. 18–19

INSINCERE

*[You are] the confirmer
of false reckonings.*

AS YOU LIKE IT

3. 4. 29

*'Tis but a base ignoble mind
That mounts no higher
than a bird can soar.*

HENRY VI, PART 2

2. 1. 13–14

*What a candy deal of courtesy
This fawning greyhound
then did proffer me!*

HENRY IV, PART 1

1. 3. 247–48

This knave's tongue begins to double.

HENRY VI, PART 2

2. 3. 89

Are you like the painting of a sorrow,
A face without a heart?

HAMLET
4. 7. 107–8

[You have] that which melteth fools—I mean
sweet words, low-crooked curtsies, and base
spaniel fawning.

JULIUS CAESAR
3. 1. 42–43

Here's an equivocator, that could swear in
both the scales against either scale.

MACBETH
2. 3. 9–10

[You are] dangerous and unsuspected.

RICHARD III
3. 5. 23

Crack the lawyer's voice,
That he may never more false title plead,
Nor sound his quillets shrilly.

TIMON OF ATHENS
4. 3. 155–57

Wilt thou whip thine own faults
in other men?

TIMON OF ATHENS
5. 1. 36–37

Though [he] is not naturally honest,
[he] is so sometimes by chance.

THE WINTER'S TALE
4. 4. 712–13

POMPOUS

If I can remember thee
I will think of thee at court.

ALL'S WELL THAT ENDS WELL
1. 1. 184–85

How ill white hairs become
a fool and jester!

HENRY IV, PART 2
5. 5. 48

There is a silly-stately style indeed!

HENRY VI, PART 1
4. 7. 72

*I am the [broom] that must sweep the court
clean of such filth as thou art.*

HENRY VI, PART 2
4. 7. 28–30

[You are] so surfeit-swell'd,
so old, and so profane.

HENRY IV, PART 2
5. 5. 50

We coldly pause for thee.

KING JOHN
2. 1. 53

Speak on sir, I dare your worst
objections: if I blush, it is to
see a nobleman want manners.

HENRY VIII
3. 2. 306–8

[He will] become the argument
of his own scorn.

MUCH ADO ABOUT NOTHING
2. 3. 11

I did never know so full a voice
issue from so empty a heart:
but the saying is true, "The empty
vessel makes the greatest sound."

HENRY V
4. 4. 69–71

*If we imagine no worse of them
than they of themselves,
they may pass for excellent men.*

THE MERRY WIVES OF WINDSOR
5. 1. 211–12

OBSTRUCTIONIST

[What] peevish opposition!

HAMLET
1. 2. 100

*[You] fortify in paper and in figures,
Using the names of men instead of men.*

HENRY IV, PART 2
1. 3. 56–57

Thou paper-faced villain.

HENRY IV, PART 2
5. 4. 11

*Go hang yourselves all: you are idle, shallow
things, I am not of your element.*

TWELFTH NIGHT
3. 4. 124–25

*[Thou art] as full of quarrel and offence as
my young mistress' dog.*

OTHELLO

2. 3. 46–47

[You] silken-coated slaves!

HENRY VI, PART 2
4. 2. 122

You are strangely troublesome.

HENRY VIII
5. 2. 128

I am sorry for thy much misgovernment.

MUCH ADO ABOUT NOTHING
4. 1. 99

INCOMPETENT

Thou art so fat-witted with drinking of old sack, and unbuttoning thee after supper, and sleeping upon benches after noon, that thou hast forgotten to demand that truly which thou wouldst truly know.

HENRY IV, PART 1
1. 2. 2–5

He is not his craft's master.

HENRY IV, PART 2
3. 2. 273

Cudgel thy brains no more about it,
for your dull ass will not mend
his pace with beating.

HAMLET
5. 1. 56–57

That such a crafty devil as his mother
should yield the world this ass!

CYMBELINE
2. 1. 54–55

[You] have done but greenly
in hugger-mugger.

HAMLET
4. 5. 83–84

When you speak best unto the purpose,
it is not worth the wagging of your beards;
and your beards deserve not so
honourable a grave as to stuff
a botcher's cushion, or to be
entombed in an ass's pack-saddle.

CORIOLANUS
2. 1. 84–87

There's no more conceit in
[you] than is in a mallet.

HENRY IV, PART 2
2. 4. 238-39

He both pleases men and angers them, and
then they laugh at him and beat him.

MUCH ADO ABOUT NOTHING
2. 1. 130-32

I may as well say the fool's a fool.

MUCH ADO ABOUT NOTHING
3. 3. 120

If [the others] be brain'd like [you],
the state totters.

THE TEMPEST
3. 2. 6

Barren practisers!

LOVE'S LABOUR'S LOST
4. 3. 322

[You are] not able to produce more accusation
Than your own weak-hing'd fancy.

THE WINTER'S TALE
2. 3. 117-18

The music of his own vain tongue
Doth ravish [him] like enchanting harmony.

LOVE'S LABOUR'S LOST
1. 1. 165–66

Image Conscious

There are a sort of men whose visages
Do cream and mantle
like a standing pond.

The Merchant of Venice
1. 1. 88–89

[Their] judgements are
Mere fathers of their garments.

All's Well That Ends Well
1. 2. 61–62

You lisp and wear strange suits.

As You Like It
4. 1. 31–32

[You] smiling pickthanks,
and base newsmongers!

Henry IV, Part 1
3. 2. 25

[There's] not an eye but is a-weary
of thy common sight.

Henry IV, Part 1
3. 2. 87–88

[You] fat, sleek-headed men!

JULIUS CAESAR
1. 2. 189–90

Observe him, for the love of mockery.

TWELFTH NIGHT
2. 5. 18–19

CONCLUSION

WE RECENTLY RECEIVED a note from a lawyer friend. He asked in a most dignified way if we would please send him a significant sum of money for a congenial two-minute telephone call we'd had. We have to confess to a certain insensitivity, for we, as authors of this seminal book on the dynamics of the legal mind, should have been more alert to the telltale signs that our friend had fallen on hard times. We could have been more responsive. After all, it is very nearly a lost virtue to maintain one's bearing in the midst of ill-fortune, what with so many people complaining these days and collapsing into baseness over the most trivial matters.

Seeing through to the deeper reasons for the dismay reflected in his letter, we telephoned him and, in the spirit of genuine regard that underlies all our writings on the profession, reassured him of the kind of respect we have for him. As we expressed our honest feelings using Shakespeare's literary genius, he began to imagine himself in rarefied company and his spirits seemed to rally.

When he writes to us again, regarding *two* two-minute calls, we are certain he will be reinvigorated, candid, and cultivated in his phrases. His improvement should be noticeable. And we, well pleased to have helped a valued friend in need, will be ready to respond again with equal generosity.